THE CAMBRIDGE BIBLE COMMENTARY

NEW ENGLISH BIBLE

GENERAL EDITORS

P. R. ACKROYD, A. R. C. LEANEY, J. W. PACKER

ISAIAH 1-39

THE BOOK OF THE PROPHET
ISAIAH

CHAPTERS 1-39

COMMENTARY BY

A. S. HERBERT

*Sometime Professor of Old Testament Studies
in the Selly Oak Colleges, Birmingham*

CAMBRIDGE

AT THE UNIVERSITY PRESS

1973

Published by the Syndics of the Cambridge University Press
Bentley House, 200 Euston Road, London NW1 2DB
American Branch: 32 East 57th Street, New York, N.Y. 10022

© Cambridge University Press 1973

Library of Congress Catalogue Card Number: 73-79495

ISBNS:
0 521 08624 8   hard cover
0 521 09766 5   paperback

Printed in Great Britain
at the University Printing House, Cambridge
(Brooke Crutchley, University Printer)

GENERAL EDITORS' PREFACE

The aim of this series is to provide the text of the New English Bible closely linked to a commentary in which the results of modern scholarship are made available to the general reader. Teachers and young people have been especially kept in mind. The commentators have been asked to assume no specialized theological knowledge, and no knowledge of Greek and Hebrew. Bare references to other literature and multiple references to other parts of the Bible have been avoided. Actual quotations have been given as often as possible.

The completion of the New Testament part of the series in 1967 provides a basis upon which the production of the much larger Old Testament and Apocrypha series can be undertaken. The welcome accorded to the series has been an encouragement to the editors to follow the same general pattern, and an attempt has been made to take account of criticisms which have been offered. One necessary change is the inclusion of the translators' footnotes since in the Old Testament these are more extensive, and essential for the understanding of the text.

Within the severe limits imposed by the size and scope of the series, each commentator will attempt to set out the main findings of recent biblical scholarship and to describe the historical background to the text. The main theological issues will also be critically discussed.

Much attention has been given to the form of the volumes. The aim is to produce books each of which will be read consecutively from first to last page. The introductory material leads naturally into the text, which itself leads into the alternating sections of the commentary.

The series is accompanied by three volumes of a more general character. *Understanding the Old Testament* sets out to provide the larger historical and archaeological background, to say something about the life and thought of the people of the Old Testament, and to answer the question 'Why should we study the Old Testament?'. *The Making of the Old Testament* is concerned with the formation of the books of the Old Testament and Apocrypha in the context of the ancient near eastern world, and with the ways in which these books have come down to us in the life of the Jewish and Christian communities. *Old Testament Illustrations* contains maps, diagrams and photographs with an explanatory text. These three volumes are designed to provide material helpful to the understanding of the individual books and their commentaries, but they are also prepared so as to be of use quite independently.

P. R. A.
A. R. C. L.
J. W. P.

CONTENTS

CONTENTS

THE FOOTNOTES TO THE
N.E.B. TEXT

The footnotes to the N.E.B. text are designed to help the reader either to understand particular points of detail – the meaning of a name, the presence of a play upon words – or to give information about the actual text. Where the Hebrew text appears to be erroneous, or there is doubt about its precise meaning, it may be necessary to turn to manuscripts which offer a different wording, or to ancient translations of the text which may suggest a better reading, or to offer a new explanation based upon conjecture. In such cases, the footnotes supply very briefly an indication of the evidence, and whether the solution proposed is one that is regarded as possible or as probable. Various abbreviations are used in the footnotes.

(1) Some abbreviations are simply of terms used in explaining a point: *ch(s).*, chapter(s); *cp.*, compare; *lit.*, literally; *mng.*, meaning; *MS(S).*, manuscript(s), i.e. Hebrew manuscript(s), unless otherwise stated; *om.*, omit(s); *or*, indicating an alternative interpretation; *poss.*, possible; *prob.*, probable; *rdg.*, reading; *Vs(s).*, Version(s).

(2) Other abbreviations indicate sources of information from which better interpretations or readings may be obtained.

Aq. Aquila, a Greek translator of the Old Testament (perhaps about A.D. 130) characterized by great literalness.

Aram. Aramaic – may refer to the text in this language (used in parts of Ezra and Daniel), or to the meaning of an Aramaic word. Aramaic belongs to the same language family as Hebrew, and is known from about 1000 B.C. over a wide area of the Middle East, including Palestine.

Heb. Hebrew – may refer to the Hebrew text or may indicate the literal meaning of the Hebrew word.

Josephus Flavius Josephus (A.D. 37/8–about 100), author of the *Jewish Antiquities*, a survey of the whole history of his people, directed partly at least to a non-Jewish audience, and of various other works, notably one on the *Jewish War* (that of A.D. 66–73) and a defence of Judaism (*Against Apion*).

Luc. Sept. Lucian's recension of the Septuagint, an important edition made in Antioch in Syria about the end of the third century A.D.

Pesh.   Peshitta or Peshitto, the Syriac version of the Old Testament. Syriac is the name given chiefly to a form of Eastern Aramaic used by the Christian community. The translation varies in quality, and is at many points influenced by the Septuagint or the Targums.

Sam.   Samaritan Pentateuch – the form of the first five books of the Old Testament as used by the Samaritan community. It is written in Hebrew in a special form of the Old Hebrew script, and preserves an important form of the text, somewhat influenced by Samaritan ideas.

Scroll(s)   Scroll(s), commonly called the Dead Sea Scrolls, found at or near Qumran from 1947 onwards. These important manuscripts shed light on the state of the Hebrew text as it was developing in the last centuries B.C. and the first century A.D.

Sept.   Septuagint (meaning 'seventy'; often abbreviated as the Roman numeral LXX), the name given to the main Greek version of the Old Testament. According to tradition, the Pentateuch was translated in Egypt in the third century B.C. by 70 (or 72) translators, six from each tribe, but the precise nature of its origin and development is not fully known. It was intended to provide Greek-speaking Jews with a convenient translation. Subsequently it came to be much revered by the Christian community.

Symm.   Symmachus, another Greek translator of the Old Testament (beginning of the third century A.D.), who tried to combine literalness with good style. Both Lucian and Jerome viewed his version with favour.

Targ.   Targum, a name given to various Aramaic versions of the Old Testament, produced over a long period and eventually standardized, for the use of Aramaic-speaking Jews.

Theod.   Theodotion, the author of a revision of the Septuagint (probably second century A.D.) very dependent on the Hebrew text.

Vulg.   Vulgate, the most important Latin version of the Old Testament, produced by Jerome about A.D. 400, and the text most used throughout the Middle Ages in western Christianity.

[…]   In the text itself square brackets are used to indicate probably late additions to the Hebrew text.

(Fuller discussion of a number of these points may be found in *The Making of the Old Testament* in this series)

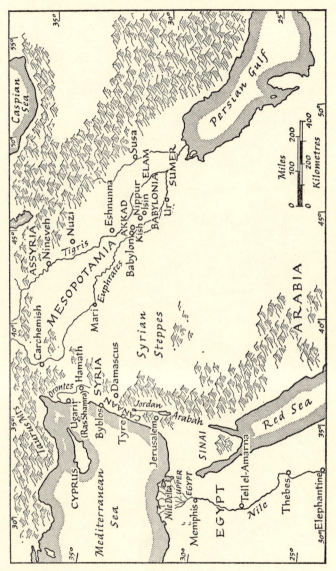

1 The Near East in Old Testament times

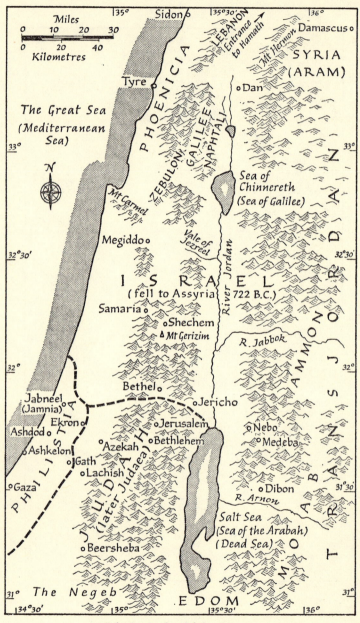

2 Palestine in the eighth century B.C.

Table of events in the eighth century B.C. bearing on Isaiah 1–39

Judah	Prophets	The Northern Kingdom	Assyria
Uzziah (Azariah) 783–742	Amos – at very end of reign of Jeroboam	Jeroboam II 786–746	Assyria weak for first half of century. A period of peace and prosperity for Israel and Judah
Jotham 742–735	Isaiah*	Zechariah 746–745. Murdered after six months' reign Shallum 745. Assassinated after one month Menahem 745–738. Accepted Assyrian sovereignty and paid heavy tribute Pekahiah 738–737. Assassinated	Tiglath-pileser 745–727. Assyria gathered strength under his rule
	Hosea probably active through most of this period	Pekah 737–732. Reversed Menahem's foreign policy. Put himself at head of anti-Assyrian coalition and attacked Judah, who had refused to join Hoshea 732–724. Murdered Pekah and surrendered to the Assyrians. But at the death of Shalmaneser re-belled again 722/1 END OF NORTHERN KINGDOM	Assyria came to Judah's aid in 732. Overthrew the other members of the coalition (Syria and Philistia) and attacked Israel
Ahaz 735–715. When attacked by Pekah and his allies, appealed for Assyrian help	Micah active for unspeci-fied period before and after fall of Samaria		Shalmaneser V 727–722
Hezekiah 715–687. Rebelled against Assyria and forced by Sennacherib to pay tribute Manasseh 687–642. Accepted Assyrian domination			Sargon II 722–705. Destroyed Samaria in 722/1 and made Israel into an Assyrian province Sennacherib 705–681. In-vaded Judah in 701, and probably again later

* Isaiah was active from the last year of Uzziah, and may have been still alive at the beginning of the reign of Manasseh.

THE BOOK OF THE PROPHET

ISAIAH

✳ ✳ ✳ ✳ ✳ ✳ ✳ ✳ ✳ ✳ ✳ ✳ ✳

THE PLACE OF THE BOOK IN
THE OLD TESTAMENT

The book of Isaiah is the first of the 'Major Prophets', so called because like the books of Jeremiah and Ezekiel, it is greater in length than the shorter 'Minor Prophets' (called 'The Twelve Prophets' in the N.E.B.). In our English Bibles, following the order of the Greek and the Latin (or Vulgate) translations, it follows the Song of Songs, which at least has the advantage of calling attention to the great variety of the Old Testament scriptures. In the Hebrew Bible, it follows directly on 2 Kings, a more natural order since this prophet was deeply involved in the historical events of his day and was concerned to give a distinctive interpretation of these events. The Rabbinic tradition in the Talmud (the 'teachings' accumulated over the centuries – see *The Making of the Old Testament*, pp. 171ff. in this series) makes Isaiah follow Jeremiah and Ezekiel. In view of the historical references in all these books this is surprising. Was it due to a recognition of the later date for chs. 40ff.? In fact the four books Joshua, Judges, Samuel and Kings are called 'The Former Prophets' while Isaiah, Jeremiah, Ezekiel and the Minor Prophets are called 'The Latter Prophets'. This draws attention to one of the distinctive features of the Old Testament, which continues into the New, i.e. its profound interest in history. This interest is not primarily in the rise and fall of kingdoms or empires, but in history as the arena of God's activity. In Law (the first five books), Prophets and Psalms, the events of history are seen as the acts of God,

I

or, more precisely, as the acts and words of Yahweh, God of Israel, who must therefore be seen as the God of the whole earth – a conclusion explicitly declared in Isaiah 40ff. Taught by her priests and prophets, Isaiah saw the events of history, past, present and future, as a living unity held together by the invincible purpose of the living God. It was the business of the prophet to discern that purpose in the events of his day, often of a disastrous character, and in the future that loomed before them. In the main, the prophets uttered words of stern condemnation and doom, for reasons that will be only too apparent when we relate their words to the conduct of their contemporaries. Even when they spoke of a glorious future, it was one that made demands upon their hearers that few would be prepared to accept. Yet history was to prove the worth of the prophetic oracles, and it was their words, cherished by their disciples, that became the source of strength and renewal when every external support had been stripped away. The prophetic confidence is well expressed by the words of Paul in Rom. 8 : 28 : 'In everything, as we know, he (the Spirit) co-operates for good with those who love God and are called according to his purpose.' It is this confidence that makes their sternest oracles not merely words of condemnation but judgements seeking penitence from those who had ears to hear, and so judgements leading to the renewal of the people of God.

THE LIFE AND TIMES OF THE PROPHET

A number of references to known historical events occur in the book. Some of these were plainly added by an editor, in order to introduce a collection of Isaiah's oracles, e.g. 1: 1; 7: 1–2; 20: 1, or the account, 36–9, largely taken from 2 Kings 18: 13 – 20: 19 which concludes this section of the book. The first of these is of too general a character to define the dates of Isaiah's ministry. The second, 7: 1f., can be dated with confidence as at the beginning of the reign of Ahaz, i.e.

about 735 B.C. (cp. 2 Kings 15: 37; 16: 5). The third, 20: 1, refers to an event not mentioned in Kings or Chronicles, but known from the Assyrian records. The revolt of the Philistine cities against Sargon, instigated by Egypt, occurred in 713 B.C. and was crushed in 711 B.C. Hezekiah of Judah was apparently not implicated. Chs. 36–9 refer to the devastating invasion by Sennacherib in 701 B.C. In addition to these we have the prophet's own account of his inaugural vision and his call to the prophetic ministry in ch. 6, 'In the year of King Uzziah's death', i.e. 742 B.C. Further, we have the prophet's account of an oracle directed against Philistia in 14: 28, in the year of King Ahaz' death, 726 B.C., and against Shebna in Isa. 22: 15–25 and the promotion of Eliakim to succeed him as chief minister. Since in 701 Eliakim held this office (Isa. 36: 3), the oracle must be dated before the Assyrian invasion. Nothing is known from the biblical records about any further activity of Isaiah after 701 B.C. The reference to his martyrdom in 'The Ascension of Isaiah', 5: 11–14, a book which contains 'The Martyrdom of Isaiah', a Jewish work written in about the first century A.D., apparently reflected in Hebrews 11: 37, is a late legend. Isaiah's ministry extended from 742 to 701 B.C., according to the Old Testament records, although we cannot rule out the possibility that his ministry continued after the latter date. Since he was married and had at least two sons by 735 B.C. (cp. Isa. 7: 3; 8: 3), we may assume that he was about twenty years old at the time of his inaugural vision and about sixty at the end of his ministry.

The period 742–701 B.C. was a tragic and critical period for Israel and Judah and is well documented both in the Bible and on Assyrian clay tablets. It was to see the destruction of the northern kingdom, together with most of the neighbouring kingdoms (cp. Isa. 37: 11–13), the invasion of Judah and its subjugation by the armies of Assyria. What had been foreseen by Amos (Amos 2: 14–16; 3: 11; 6: 7, 14; 9: 8), and more clearly, because in part experienced, by Hosea (Hos. 5: 8–12; 7: 11–13; 9: 3; 10: 14; 11: 5f.; 13: 16; 14: 1), became a terrible reality in the days of Micah and Isaiah. Some understanding of the international situation in the latter half of the eighth century is essential if we are to do justice to Isaiah's oracles, for supremely among the eighth-century prophets, he betrays an acute perception of the issues involved. Certainly his interests were not merely in politics, but in the relationship between God and his people. Yet, as he saw it, this relationship, or more precisely the defection from it on the part of the people (Isa. 1: 2), was not simply a matter of 'religious' observance but one that had implications and consequences in the political situation. Isaiah has been described as the statesman–prophet, but his statesmanship was the product of his overriding concern with the will of God in this world. Like all the 'goodly fellowship of the prophets', Isaiah was a man of the world because he was a man of God.

The death of the kings Jeroboam II of Israel (746/5 B.C.) and Uzziah of Judah (742) brought to an end a period of security and prosperity for the two states. The decline of Israel was hastened by the outbreak of civil war, which, with brief intermissions, was to last for the next twenty years and ended with the total subjugation of that kingdom by the Assyrian armies in 721. The more stable government of the southern kingdom, together with the fact of its relative insignificance politically and economically, made it possible for it to survive, though with a loss of independence, under Ahaz (2 Kings 16: 10–18), and of most of its territory except that of the city-state of Jerusalem under Hezekiah (cp. Isa. 1: 7–8 and Sennacherib's inscription). But the fate of the Israelite kingdoms was part of a much larger process in which a resurgent and vigorous Assyria was expanding its empire and contesting the declining power of Egypt, which for long had claimed the Asiatic kingdoms at the eastern end of the Mediterranean as its sphere of influence. Egypt was in fact in no position to exert this influence or help in the defence of these states since its kingdom had disintegrated into a number of rival states, and its only policy was to defend the borders

4

of Egypt to the last Israelite, Judaean, Philistine etc. By reason both of its internal dissensions and of its cynical foreign policy, Isaiah dismissed reliance on Egypt as folly (31: 1–3); the Assyrian commander in 36: 6 is no less scathing: 'Egypt is a splintered cane that will run into a man's hand and pierce it if he leans on it.' It was, however, very difficult for the statesmen of the little kingdoms in this part of the world to decide where their advantage lay. Egypt, although its power was waning, was close at hand. Assyria was far away (Isa. 5: 26) and its empire by no means secure. Yet, as events were to show, the day of small independent kingdoms was at an end.

The process began under Tiglath-pileser III (745–727) who came to the Assyrian throne after a long period of weakness in the Mesopotamian Empire. In a series of campaigns he rapidly subjugated the kingdoms on his borders and proceeded to extend his empire to the west. Israel was in no condition to resist, for the kingdom, after the death of Jeroboam II, was rent by civil war (2 Kings 15: 8–28); one adventurer after another seized the throne after murdering his predecessor. The consequences for the life of the Israelite society are made terribly clear in 2 Kings 15: 16 and throughout much of the book of Hosea. When the Assyrian armies advanced on Israel, Menahem could do no more than surrender and pay tribute (2 Kings 15: 19), probably hoping that he would be supported on the throne by his overlord. His son, Pekahiah, was murdered by Pekah apparently with the intention of declaring independence. Pekah, in a desperate attempt to resist Assyria, made an alliance with Rezin of Damascus and sought to compel Ahaz of Judah to join them (2 Kings 15: 37) and if he would not, to depose him and set 'the son of Tabeal' (an Aramean?) in his place (Isa. 7: 1–6). In spite of the warnings of Isaiah, Ahaz saw no other way than to appeal to Tiglath-pileser for help, and in doing so became a vassal state of the Assyrian Empire. In any case Tiglath-pileser could not tolerate the defection of Pekah and Rezin. By 732, the two kingdoms were subjugated. Most of Israel was turned into Assyrian provinces.

Pekah was murdered by Hoshea, and the latter was apparently rewarded by being allowed to rule, as vassal, over Ephraim and western Manasseh. Some years later, after the death of Tiglath-pileser, Hoshea defected, relying on Egyptian help. It was a disastrous move and under Sargon II (722–705) Samaria was conquered and the northern kingdom ceased to exist (721). According to the Assyrian records, 27,290 Israelites were deported, numerically a small proportion of the population, but obviously including any likely to cause disaffection (2 Kings 17: 4–6).

Judah escaped the ravages inflicted on the northern kingdom, but at grave cost. 2 Kings 16: 10–18 implies that as a mark of his political subservience, Ahaz had to accept his overlord's gods, and the rituals associated with them. The evidence is not in fact clear, since what is described is Syrian rather than Assyrian. During his reign also there was a recrudescence of Canaanite religious practices (2 Kings 16: 3–4; cp. Isa. 2: 6–8). In addition the country was affected economically. It had lost territory (2 Kings 16: 6) and had to pay heavy tribute (2 Kings 16: 8, 17). Both Isaiah and Micah present a picture of grave deterioration in society. Yet during the reign of Ahaz and the earlier part of Hezekiah's reign, the country was untroubled by the enemies of Assyria, so long as it remained loyal. There was discontent and resentment, which was to manifest itself in Hezekiah's reign. Part of this was caused by the heavy taxation to meet the Assyrian tribute. While this affected directly the nobles, merchants and country magnates, indirectly the effect was felt by the peasant farmers and the rural population of Judah. Resentment of Judaean dependence on Assyria could hardly fail to be excited whenever such psalms as 72 and 110 were recalled, or Passover was celebrated. Deeper than all this was the intolerable subordination of the religion of Yahweh to that of other deities in the Jerusalem temple. While the full implications of this subordination were doubtless apparent to such prophets as Isaiah and Micah, the offence was felt by many loyal priests and worshippers. If, as seems probable, it was during this period that refugee Levites had brought with them the ancient traditions of the northern shrines and disciples of the prophets had come with the oracles of Amos and Hosea, we can understand the readiness for reform that marked the reign of Hezekiah (2 Kings 18: 4; cp. 2 Chron. 29–31). But such a re-assertion of Yahweh in the state religion was in itself a rebellion against the empire (2 Kings 18: 7*b*). During the first ten years of the reign of Sargon II (722–705) this was only possible as that king was involved in major campaigns to the north and east of his empire. Within the empire itself, Babylon successfully declared independence under Marduk-apal-iddina (Isa. 39: 1 Merodach-baladan), and in the south Egypt was united under the vigorous Twenty-Fifth Dynasty.

The time seemed ripe for open rebellion, and with the promise of Egyptian aid Ashdod openly revolted in 714. It is not quite clear how far Judah was involved, but apparently Isaiah's vigorous warning (Isa. 20) was sufficient to cause hesitation and when Ashdod was crushed by Sargon's army, Judah was not invaded. But the death of Sargon in battle (705) was followed by widespread revolts, fomented by Marduk-apal-idinna of Babylon and Shabako of Egypt. This time, in spite of Isaiah's warnings (Isa. 30 and 31), Hezekiah joined the rebels, and prepared for the defence of the city by constructing the Siloam tunnel (2 Kings 20: 20; cp. Isa. 22: 8–11), to provide a water-supply within the city. Retribution was inevitable. Neither his own defences, nor the support of his allies, nor the help promised by Egypt could prevent the invasion by Sennacherib. The Assyrian armies brought destruction upon forty-six of Judah's fortified cities, killing many of their inhabitants and deporting others. Jerusalem itself was besieged and, to quote Sennacherib's description, 'Hezekiah, the Jew,...I shut up like a caged bird within Jerusalem, his royal city.' The siege ended with Hezekiah's total submission, increased tribute, the surrender of his daughters to his conqueror and the loss of most of his territory (2 Kings 18: 13–16).

The Assyrian records referring to this and other events of the period are available in *Ancient Near Eastern Texts* or *Documents from Old Testament Times* – see Note on Further Reading). So far as the biblical records show, the year 701 is the end of Isaiah's ministry.

Of the prophet himself we know nothing beyond what is recorded or can be inferred from his book. His work was conducted mainly or entirely in Jerusalem. Isaiah's presence in the temple at the time of his inaugural vision should be noted. For the Jerusalem temple was not, in our sense of the word, a place of public worship. It was the shrine of the kingdom in the sense that there the sacrifices and rituals were performed, notably by the king, for and on behalf of the people in order to secure the divine blessing. It was there, in the Most Holy Place, the inner shrine, that the Ark was kept. Isaiah's presence there suggests that he was a privileged person, either a recognized prophet attached to the shrine or a member of the court circle. His ease of access to the king (Ahaz 7: 3ff.; Hezekiah 37: 21f.; 38: 1–8; 39: 5–8) his relationship with state officials (8: 2; 22: 15–25) would indicate this. The content of his message suggests a familiarity with the liturgy of the temple; there are points of resemblance between his language, especially his frequent use of the word 'holy', and that of Lev. 17–26, apparently the temple *torah* (which sets out what was required in ritual and conduct from the priests of the Jerusalem temple) or at least based on the *torah*. He obviously had inside knowledge of state policy (30: 1–2; 37: 14ff.; 39: 1–4), and was keenly aware of the international politics of his day. He was married to a woman who was described as a prophetess (8: 3), and had at least two sons (7: 3; 8: 3) by the year 734 B.C. His ministry appears to have been exercised solely in Jerusalem or its immediate neighbourhood. There are obvious points of resemblance between Isaiah's oracles against social injustices and those of Amos, and between Isaiah's references to the political turmoil in the northern kingdom and those of Hosea. In neither case, however, would

8

it be possible to say that Isaiah knew directly of the work of those two prophets. We might feel that it is surprising that he makes no reference to the work of his great contemporary Micah (about 725–701 B.C.); the inclusion of the words in Isa. 2: 2–4 = Mic. 4: 1–3 may be due to other factors (see the comment on those passages). But this may be accounted for by the fact that the two prophets moved in quite different circles, socially and geographically, and in any case the means of communication in the ancient world were very different from ours. The most important factor in Isaiah's life was his temple-vision. Whatever may have been his manner of life beforehand, this was the turning point, a radical 'conversion', and, like the experience of Jeremiah in Jer. 1: 4–10, or that of Paul in Acts 9: 1–19, it was an event that profoundly affected his life and message. It was, as he himself describes it, a shattering experience, a death and a rebirth, through which he was able to see the death and rebirth of his people.

PROPHECY

Isaiah was a prophet. To say that, however, tells us very little, since the term prophet is variously used in English and commonly in a sense that is by no means always applicable to the work of Isaiah or indeed of any other of the prophets whose words are recorded in the Old Testament. For the noun 'prophet' and the verb 'prophesy' in English commonly emphasize foretelling the future, prediction. Undoubtedly the prophets of the Old Testament did predict. Yet prediction occupies a smaller place in their oracles than our usage would lead us to expect. Furthermore, their predictions were such in a very special sense, and intimately related to their understanding of the 'Word of the LORD'. Again, the word 'prophet' is used both in the Old Testament and in the world in which Israel lived with considerable variety of meaning. The 400 men in 1 Kings 22 are called prophets, as is Micaiah. The abnormal behaviour of Saul in 1 Sam. 19: 24 led men to describe him as a prophet, but this behaviour would hardly be characteristic of Isaiah, even though for a particular occasion he went about as a prisoner of war (Isa. 20: 2-4). Prophecy was a well-known phenomenon in the ancient Near East. From the eighteenth-century B.C. kingdom of Mari on the Middle Euphrates we learn of a 'man of the god Dagan' who was directed to go to the king with the words, 'Go...thou shalt say...'; cp. Isa. 22: 15. There are important points of resemblance between these prophets and the prophets of the Old Testament, yet the difference between them and so many who are called prophets in the Old Testament on the one hand, and that remarkable succession of prophets beginning with Moses (Deut. 18: 15), and continuing through Israel's history with Elijah, Amos etc., on the other is unmistakable. These latter were men of very varied temperament, background and experience, but wherever we have any information about their initiatory experience, we find them under a constraint that was for them inescapable. They were called, perhaps summoned would be a better word, by Yahweh, who chose Israel to be his people when Israel was a slave people in Egypt. The one who called, no less than the experience of vocation, is what gives the distinctive character to Israel's great prophets. These men were called by God to perform a particular task in the life of his people, and through his people in the life of mankind. Few would dispute the statement that the prophets of the Old Testament occupy a central place in the religion of Israel and in the spiritual development of mankind. Can we define more exactly what is meant by the word 'prophet'?

To recapitulate: to the modern mind the word prophet suggests one who foretells future events. This is not the primary or essential meaning either of the Greek from which the English word derives, or of the Hebrew which it translates. Certainly the prophets did make predictions, yet these predictions were commonly of the imminent future and closely related to present conduct or circumstances. Prediction in this sense is a necessary element in prophecy. Occasionally the prophet will look to the more distant future, especially as he sees the divine judgement issuing into the work of renewal and salvation (cp. Isa. 1: 24–8). There is, however, nothing mechanical or automatic about these predictions. It is the prophet's work to declare 'the word of the LORD'. It is, indeed, one of the characteristic phrases of the prophetic utterance: 'these are the words of the Lord' (10: 24), 'says the LORD' (30: 1), 'the LORD has spoken' (1: 2), 'the LORD said' (3: 16). This is not merely the expression of an idea, or the conveying of information. It expresses the will of God, which, coming into the life of the world through the prophet, brings about that which it declares. The clearest expression of this may be found at Isa. 55: 11 where the word is described as going from God's mouth to prevail and to accomplish his will. It may be described as God in his outgoing activity. This word, received and declared by the prophet, operates in the lives of those who hear, to effect the divine purpose. It is described by Jeremiah (23: 29) as a hammer that shatters the rocks, or as creating the world in Ps. 33: 9, or healing and saving in Ps. 107: 20.

Prediction then is the description of what will be as the result of the divine energy released into the world through the prophetic utterance. The word of the Lord works through the lives and activities of men towards its own fulfilment by the inherent energy of him who spoke. Predominantly, the prophetic oracles were oracles of doom directed to those who had rebelled against God. Yet this is a situation in which persons, divine and human, are involved. The oracle of doom will be fulfilled, unless there is a change in the lives of those who hear. This means that prediction must be conditional. This is finely portrayed in the story of Jonah, who knew that his word of doom on Nineveh would be averted at the first hint of repentance. This is apparent in most of the books of the prophets. The very purpose in the oracle that foretells doom is that it may penetrate the hardened heart and awaken Israel to its true place within the divine purpose, in order that in penitence it may live and not die (cp. Amos 5: 6, 14). Perhaps we should rather see the oracles of doom, terrifying and apparently absolute though they are, as a parenthesis within the divine blessing uttered by Moses, and its fulfilment more or less clearly apprehended by all the prophets, but most clearly in Isa. 40–55.

Important as is the element of foretelling in the prophetic ministry, it is by no means the whole, and it is not specifically the meaning of the Hebrew word for prophet, *nābī'*. The exact significance of the word may be in doubt, although it appears to be connected with an Accadian word *nābū*, meaning to call or announce. What is less certain is the significance to be attached to the form of the word in Hebrew. It might mean simply 'one who is called (by God)', but this would seem to be too general, since, though the prophets give every indication of being called, the same could be said of others, e.g. Gideon, David. It could mean 'one who announces' and, specifically, 'a message that he has received'. This is of course true of Israel's prophets, and suits the ascription of the word prophet to Aaron in Exod. 7: 1 (cp. Exod. 4: 15f.). Two other words are used of prophets, *ḥōzeh* and *rō'eh* both meaning 'one who sees', 'a seer'. Indeed the verb *ḥāzāh*, 'he saw', is used in Isaiah 2: 1, 'received in a vision' (literally 'saw'). This may be part of a later editorial note (cp. Isa. 1: 1) but it may indicate that the prophet was one who saw what others failed to see. It should be noted, however, that when Isaiah describes his inaugural vision, he uses the quite common verb for seeing (6: 1). Further we must note that the prophets themselves use the word *nābī'*, without adjective, for those whom we should call false prophets: Isa. 3: 2; Jer. 28; Ezek. 13: 3f. A study of the language does not greatly help us to understand the nature of prophecy except to suggest a heightened perception of spiritual reality which may indeed have been present, in however perverted a form, in the 'false' prophets. Clearly an important human factor in prophecy is the absolute trust and loyal obedience of the prophet (cp. Deut. 13: 1–5), at whatever cost, to the God who has entrusted his word to his servant. This is especially apparent in the record of Jeremiah's experience, but easily recognizable in other prophets.

Attention has been drawn of recent years to guilds of persons attached to, or associated with, the shrines, who were called prophets; cp. 1 Sam. 10: 5–13. These are commonly described as 'sons of the prophets' (2 Kings 2: 3, 5, 7; translated 'company of prophets' in the N.E.B.). Sometimes prophets and priests are referred to as though they were closely associated (Mic. 3: 11; Jer. 6: 13; 23: 11 etc.). It is probable, then, that these prophets were associated with shrines where they could be consulted in some emergency (cp. 1 Kings 14: 2). It has been suggested that the great prophets of the Old Testament were members of the shrine personnel. This would seem to be pressing the evidence too far. Certainly Amos prophesied at Bethel, but it is hardly likely that he belonged to that shrine in any official capacity; it was simply the most appropriate place at which he would meet the leaders, including the priests, of Israel. Isaiah received his inaugural vision in the temple (6: 1), and like other prophets, knew a good deal about the practices taking place in the temple (1: 11ff.), and had direct access to the king (7: 3ff.; 38: 1) and was consulted by King Hezekiah (37: 2). On two of these occasions the prophetic word was of an exclusively political character, like that of the prophets who counselled the king of Israel in 1 Kings 22: 5f., but it would be going beyond the evidence to argue from this that Isaiah's ministry was that of one of the 'official' prophets. Whatever be the origin of Israelite prophecy, the difference between the eighth-century prophets, or for that matter their predecessors like Nathan and Elijah, and contemporary 'prophets' is of such a degree as to be a difference in kind. Nowhere else do we find such perception of spiritual reality or moral values as we find in this remarkable succession.

At the occasion of his vision in the temple, Isaiah's lips were touched with a coal from the altar, in order that, thus purged of the impurity of sin, they might utter the divine oracles. He became God's messenger. As such he became, in a highly suggestive phrase, an extension of God's personality. The message that he gives, the judgement that he utters, is not his, the prophet's, but God's own words. This is well brought out in Isa. 32: 9–20, where the first person pronoun could refer either to God or the prophet or to both. Whatever explanation we offer, the prophet has so identified himself, or has been so fully taken into the divine counsel (or council, for the one Hebrew word is used for both the English words; cp. Amos 3: 7; Jer. 23: 18, 22), that he is at one with the divine king. He was chosen by God for this purpose; he was God's man. Yet the claim of God is personally realized, and the response of the prophet must be given if the divine will is to be actualized in the life of man. For the prophet is still a man of Israel, one of the covenant community, and it is this relationship that determines the form of his message. He is 'among a people of unclean lips', at the very centre of their life and sensitive to their whole life with all its rebellion and iniquity. When therefore he utters the divine word of doom, it is in his own life, organically representative of Israel, that that doom is realized. And his own repentance is an acted symbol of the repentance of Israel and generating that movement of the will in the life of his people. He is bound to them, God's people, in a solidarity of life. God and his people meet in the life of the prophet.

(THE MESSAGE OF ISAIAH)

It may be misleading to speak of the theology of this prophet, since, even if we could reconstruct a chronological order for his oracles, we should not find a systematic presentation of the ways of God with men. Clearly the form of his teaching is conditioned by the historical circumstances in which he lived, the rise to power of Assyria in the latter half of the eighth century B.C., and the effect of that on the kingdoms of

Israel and Judah. But the content is that which is already present in his inaugural vision, ch. 6, and is worked out through the various situations which the prophet met. Yahweh is the Holy One of Israel, the exalted king who governs not only the affairs of those who lived in Canaan, but the affairs of the nations – even Egypt and Assyria. The only appropriate response of man is humility, repentance, and exclusive trust, and this is to be manifested within the political and social circumstances in which men live. If, then, we speak of the theology of Isaiah of Jerusalem, it is a very practical theology; what God is like has immediate consequences for man in relation to his fellows, and to his attitude to political affairs. The Holy One of Israel is down-to-earth transcendence. He who is unapproachable by men, approaches man in the daily affairs of life, in his social and political life no less than in the solemn acts of worship. The understanding of God presented by this prophet is among the most sublime in the Old Testament. It is also, in all its sublimity, firmly related to such mundane matters as international politics, the life of society and the daily conduct (or misconduct) of men.

The phrase 'The Holy One of Israel' is characteristic of the book of Isaiah. It occurs twelve times in chs. 1–39 and thirteen times in chs. 40–66. We may also add 'his (Israel's) Holy One', 10: 17; 49: 7; 'the Holy One of Jacob', 29: 23; and 'your Holy One', 43: 15. Elsewhere in the Old Testament, the phrase occurs only in Ps. 71: 22; 78: 41; 89: 18 (19); Jer. 50: 29; 51: 5; and 2 Kings 19: 22 (= Isa. 37: 23). The use of this phrase in Isaiah appears to derive from the antiphonal hymn heard by the prophet in his inaugural vision (6: 3). If the manifest content of the vision is to be found in the ritual words and acts of the Jerusalem temple, then we may see the origin of the phrase in the liturgy of the temple. This is supported by its use in the psalms. The word 'holy' is primarily not an ethical term, but one indicating the otherness, the incalculable power, of God, his inaccessibility. He is 'the great stranger in the human world' (G. von Rad, *Old Testa-*

6-3

ment Theology, vol. 1, p. 205 – see Note on Further Reading). That is what makes the use of the phrase throughout this book so striking a paradox. Although not primarily a term meaning moral perfection, in the thinking of Israel it was implicitly so because of Yahweh's ethical character. It became explicitly so in the teaching of Isaiah in the striking words of Isa. 5: 16 'by righteousness the holy God shows himself holy'. It is this that impels the prophet to declare himself lost, when confronted by the holy God (6: 5), and so to see the real horror of the situation for a sinful and rebellious Israel whose God is the Holy One. Both righteousness and justice are terms in the Old Testament which have connotations far wider than the ethical and legal meanings that we attach to them. They are terms of relationship indicating activity that maintains or restores the strength and welfare of the community. Thus righteousness may be used as a parallel term for saving acts (Ps. 71: 15) and justice is seen as the outcome of the divine pity (Isa. 30: 18). Righteousness and justice relate especially to the concept of the covenant relationship, particularly in Isaiah to the covenant created by God with the Davidic line (9: 7; 11: 3–5). Whereas in the pre-prophetic period the divine righteousness was seen as protecting Israel from the attacks of external enemies, the prophets see oppression and the perversion of justice within Israel as confronting evil-doers in Israel with the divine righteousness.

The 'glory' of God, the self-manifestation of his rule and power, fills the whole earth. Thus wherever men act in opposition to the holy God they bring destruction upon themselves (cp. 2: 12–22) while the appropriate response of man is faith (cp. 30: 15). This 'faith' has quite practical implications and is particularly required in relation to the politics of the eighth century B.C. Judah should not be fearful of the attacks by Ephraim and Syria (7: 1–9) nor seek foreign aid from Assyria (7: 10–20; 8: 5–15) or Egypt (30: 1–7; 31: 1–3). Failure to trust in God can only lead to disaster and it is the urgent plea of Isaiah that his people should return to him in humble penitence (30: 15; 31: 6). It is the prophet's sensitiveness to the (to him) manifest rule of the Holy One of Israel, that compels him to expose the evil conduct of his contemporaries. His moving description of them as those whom God has treated as sons, who have rebelled and become incredibly senseless and without understanding, is the background against which his denunciation must be read. The holy God looked for justice and righteousness but found gross injustice and oppression (5: 7). Then Isaiah describes in more detail the kind of conduct which evokes his agonized cry 'Shame on you!' in 5: 8–23; 10: 1–4. He sees the land-grabbers dispossessing the poor, the drunkards too stupefied to recognize divine activity, the cynical, conceited, perverters of justice, and gross misgovernment by the leaders of the nation. Such conduct is a flagrant denial of God and can only encounter his wrath (2: 12–21). The conclusion would seem to be the utter annihilation of Israel (5: 24–5). Here we meet with the religiously conditional element in the prophet's words. It appears in his use of the term 'remnant'. Taken by itself the word means simply a few survivors in a scene of destruction (2 Sam. 21: 2; Amos 9: 12 (N.E.B. 'what is left'); Jer. 25: 20). When Isaiah took his son with the symbolic name Shear-Jashub (a remnant shall return), the verses in 7: 18–25 make it evident that it was in this sense that he used the word 'remnant'. In ch. 10, verses 18–19 also use the word remnant in this sense. The name was one of ill-omen, like that of his younger son Maher-shalal-hash-baz in 8: 1–4, and it is to be compared with what is said in 1: 9; 17: 6. Yet there is an ambiguity in the word which made it possible to turn the word of doom into a word of hope. A remnant shall survive to turn again to God (10: 21–2; 37: 31–2).

The thought of a surviving remnant, purified and restored, may be related to Isaiah's distinctive teaching about Zion and, to a lesser extent, the Davidic dynasty. It may be noted that this prophet has little to say about the exodus from Egypt and the covenant of Sinai which play an important part in the other eighth-century prophets. The place of these concepts is taken by Zion (Jerusalem) and the covenant with the Davidic king (cp. 2 Sam. 23: 1–7). The place of Zion in the religion of the temple may be seen in Pss. 46, 48, 76, where God mysteriously defeats the armies' attack. It is reasonable to suppose that such language formed part of the mental furniture of Isaiah, who also speaks of a mysterious deliverance (cp. Isa. 17: 12–14). The vivid description of the advance of the Assyrian armies is followed by a dramatic intervention by God (10: 28–34). Similar passages may be found in relation to the attack by Sennacherib in Isa. 29: 5–8; 30: 27–33; 31: 1–8.

It should be said that Isaiah's use of the ancient traditions about Zion modifies them considerably. In 29: 1–4 God is the besieger of Ariel (Zion) – his sacrificial altar. In the thought of Isaiah's contemporaries, Jerusalem was inviolable; God would never abandon it. They were at ease in Zion. But the governors of this 'faithful' city had replaced righteousness and justice with murder, robbery, bribery and a callous disregard for the condition of the defenceless widow and orphan (1: 21–3). They have ceased to trust him who alone can preserve Zion inviolate (31: 1). By their conduct they have made an enemy of their only protector (3: 13, 14; 30: 11), and that can only mean irretrievable disaster. Their state and their fate is like that of Sodom and Gomorrah (1: 10). The great sacrifices whereby men sought communion with God and power from on high were an affront to the Holy One while they lived in defiance of his will. Prayer itself was worse than useless unless it was offered in the spirit that moved the prophet himself (1: 11–17) and accompanied by a radical change in conduct. In other words Zion must know what the prophet himself had experienced, that she is lost until in penitence she seeks and receives the forgiveness of sins. Until then she can only see God as enemy and alien, performing 'how strange a deed...how outlandish a work' (28: 21). Yet beyond that 'he is waiting to show you his favour', yearning 'to have pity on you'; see Isa. 30: 18. In contrast to the theme 'Jerusalem must be destroyed' is the hope, partially realized in the invasion of Sennacherib in 701 B.C., that Jerusalem will be saved (14: 32; 29: 5-7; 37: 31-5). There is no contradiction here between the justice and mercy of God. Judgement is fulfilled when life is renewed. The renewal of life will be seen when injustice and violence are removed (1: 25-7; 29: 19-21; 32: 16), and replaced with good government and justice (32: 1-8).

Obviously connected with the theme of Jerusalem who must be destroyed in order to be renewed, is the theme of the Davidic king. This must be considered against the background of thought, particularly in the Jerusalem temple, of the significance of the anointed king in the relationship between God and his people. It will be sufficient for our purpose to refer to 2 Sam. 7: 1-17; 23: 1-7; and many of the psalms which relate to God's anointed e.g. 2, 20, 21, 72, 89, 110, 132. (For a fuller treatment of this see on p. 216 the commentary on *Psalms* by J. H. Eaton, and A. R. Johnson, *Sacral Kingship in Ancient Israel*.) Such passages draw attention to the divine choice of the dynasty, the everlasting covenant, the obligation laid upon the king to maintain righteousness and the well-being of his people, the gift of Spirit and the assurance of divine protection and victory. It is this view of kingship which Isaiah inherited from his Jerusalem background. Of the two kings, Ahaz and Hezekiah, it is evident that the former, both by his lack of faith and his subservience to Assyria even in matters of religion on the one hand and the corrupt manner of his government on the other, could not meet the requirements expected of the anointed of God. Even Hezekiah, although he was certainly one of the better kings of Judah (cp. 2 Kings 18: 3-7), wavered in his loyalty to God (cp. Isa. 39: 1-8). It is not surprising therefore that Isaiah uttered words of condemnation against the king. Yet he retained the conviction expressed in the liturgies that kingship was part of the divine purpose. The passages immediately related to this faith are 7: 14-16; 9: 2-7 (1-6); 11: 1-9; 32: 1-8. Of these the first is quite precisely dated as being spoken to Ahaz at a time of acute political crisis; the last is of a more general character and may be an expansion of an original word of the prophet. The remaining two passages appear to be based on some part of a royal liturgy, perhaps an enthronement liturgy, and adapted to meet the prophetic insight. The first, the Immanuel prophecy, refers to the immediate future. A child (? of the royal line) is about to be born, and bearing the symbolic name will bring about a reign in Judah that, unlike that of Ahaz, will be marked by faith in the presence and activity of God. The main emphasis is on what God is already doing, which Ahaz refuses to acknowledge, for the salvation of his people. The second passage is also related to a particular situation, namely the annexation of the northern part of Israel into his empire. The conqueror's burdensome yoke will be broken by God's intervention; then the government will be given, apparently of the whole land, to a king who shall fully realize all that was associated with the name David. In 11:1–9 the anointed king is, like David, equipped with the Spirit in order effectively to discharge his rule, and to establish true justice (cp. 2 Sam. 23:3; Ps. 72:12–14). This will bring about a great transformation of the world order in which all the destructive aspects of nature will come to an end; there will be universal prosperity, because all, man and nature, will acknowledge the sovereignty of God ('knowledge of the Lord', 11:9). When man is reconciled with God, the reconciliation affects also God's handiwork, the world of nature.

What Isaiah had to say about the divine work of judgement and deliverance inevitably had its bearing on his consideration of nations beyond Israel. This is no new thing, since Amos had also uttered his word of the Lord against the nations contiguous with Israel. But the historical situation in which Isaiah was involved made it necessary for this to be extended, until in the world-view of the people of his day, the whole inhabited world is brought within the purview of divine judgement. In his inaugural vision, the prophet saw the divine glory, the divine majesty, as filling the whole earth. Not only the neighbouring nations, such as Syria, Philistia, Moab and Edom, but Egypt, Ethiopia and especially Assyria, the dominant power in international politics, are seen in terms of God's sovereign power. The imperial ambitions of Assyria are referred to, not in terms of power politics, but as God's judgement on Israel (10: 5ff.), yet when its imperial pride overreached itself, it too must be humbled (10: 12–19). The attempt on the part of Egypt to involve the small nations against Assyria in order to stave off the Assyrian attack, brings that nation also under judgement (19: 1–15; 31: 3). In fact the whole world is involved 'in that day'. The prophet does not explicitly say that Yahweh alone is God, but it is evident, from what he does say, that there is no room for any other. The gods are no more than worthlessness ('idols', 10: 10): Yahweh alone is King.

THE STRUCTURE OF ISAIAH 1–39

These chapters divide into four main sections:

A. 1–12. Oracles about Judah and Jerusalem, mainly of a threatening character (1–11) with a doxology (12).

B. 13–27. Oracles against the nations (13–23) with a conclusion consisting of prophecies and psalms relating to a final act of judgement (24–7).

C. 28–35. Oracles about Samaria and Jerusalem (28–32) followed by a psalm-like chapter (33) and a conclusion describing the final judgement on the nations and restoration of Jerusalem (34–5).

D. 36–9. Historical appendix, mainly repeating 2 Kings 18: 13 – 20: 19).

These sections are so distinct that it is possible to think of each of the first three as a separate collection of oracles which were subsequently brought together, and that D was added to an original book of prophetic oracles. It is evident, too, that each of these collections has been formed from smaller units, and it would appear that the oracles of the prophet were preserved among different groups of his disciples, each of whom added to the words of the eighth-century prophet oracles and psalms which they felt to be appropriate. It will be noticed that, in each section, the concluding oracles and psalms contain words of salvation and consolation. This arrangement of threats and promises is to be found in other prophetic collections. Since some of these concluding passages, notably 24–7 and 34–5, are manifestly of a date later than the eighth century B.C., this arrangement may be seen as the deliberate work of the continuing community of Isaiah's disciples. An interesting example of this arrangement of threat leading to promise of salvation may be found at the close of the book of Isaiah where Jewish tradition requires that, when ch. 66 is read, verse 23 should be repeated after verse 24 in order that the reading should end with a promise.

THE TEXT

A particular interest in the book of Isaiah arises from the fact that in the caves of the Judaean desert at Qumran towards the northern end of the Dead Sea, a complete copy of the book was discovered and part of another copy, together with some fragments of a commentary. These are all of a pre-Christian date and therefore bear witness to the Hebrew text, which existed about 1000 years earlier than that which is represented in our Hebrew Bibles, i.e. the text preserved by the Jewish scholars called the Masoretes. The complete scroll of Isaiah found in the Qumran cave contains a number of readings which differ from the Masoretic text, and appears to belong to a tradition which was probably used by the Jewish scholars who translated the book of Isaiah into Greek (the Septuagint). The incomplete scroll found in the Qumran cave contains only fragments of chs. 1–39, but most of chs. 41–66; this scroll agrees more closely with the Masoretic text. It is evident that the text of Isaiah has been preserved with remarkable fidelity through the many generations of copying. There are, of course, occasions where errors have occurred and the scroll can help to clear up obscurities. Examples appear in the N.E.B. footnotes (cp. 8: 2; 18: 7).

Isaiah was translated into Greek in about 200 B.C. and this, with the rest of the Bible in Greek, is known as the Septuagint. This translation must be used with caution since its rendering of Isaiah is often very free, and also was evidently made from a text which differed from the Masoretic text. There are, however, passages where it is helpful in restoring the text which has suffered in the course of transmission, as at 9: 7 and 11: 1. Occasional references are made to the Vulgate, Jerome's Latin translation (15: 5 footnote *d*) and to the Peshitta or Syriac translation (5: 19 footnote *c*).

There remain some passages in which the Hebrew text as it stands has suffered in the process of copying, apparently before the great care exercised by the Masoretes began. An example may be found at 10: 5, where the literal translation of the second clause would be 'and the staff it is in their hand my wrath.' Here N.E.B. has produced an intelligible sentence mainly by changing the order of the Hebrew words. Another example of such conjectural emendation may be found at 28: 1.

✻   ✻   ✻   ✻   ✻   ✻   ✻   ✻   ✻   ✻   ✻   ✻

Judah arraigned

THE TITLE

THE VISION received by Isaiah son of Amoz concerning **1** Judah and Jerusalem during the reigns of Uzziah, Jotham, Ahaz, and Hezekiah, kings of Judah.

✻ 1. This heading was given by the editor of the collections of Isaiah's oracles, probably to the collection in chapters 1–12, which mainly relate to *Judah and Jerusalem*. While the verb (*received*) and noun (*vision*) occur in all parts of the Old Testament (especially in Psalms and Job), they are most frequently used in Isaiah and Ezekiel. *vision* occurs also as a title in Nahum 1: 1; Obad. 1: 1; cp. 2 Chron. 32: 32; while the corresponding verb appears in Isa. 2: 1; Amos 1: 1; Mic. 1: 1. As the word is used, it corresponds to the more general English usage of 'revelation', and is often associated with revelations of the End in Daniel. This heading defines the period of the prophet's ministry, i.e. during the last forty years of the eighth century B.C. ✳

THE INDICTMENT

2   Hark you heavens, and earth give ear,
            for the LORD has spoken:
         I have sons whom I reared and brought up,
         but they have rebelled against me.
3   The ox knows its owner
            and the ass its master's stall;
         but Israel, my own people,
         has no knowledge, no discernment.

✳ 2–3. The mode of speech is that of the law-court, in which the great king summons his people for senselessly rebelling against him, although he has treated them as his own children. Their behaviour is quite irrational and unnatural. The Hebrew word-order, even more than the printed English, suggests the strong emotional reaction of horror: it is *sons*. . . 'children' (verse 4). . .*Israel*. . .*my own people* who *have rebelled*. Further, the language recalls the language of Exod. 3: 10; 4: 22–3, where the Lord acted to deliver 'my people Israel', 'my first born son'. Hosea used the same language (1: 10; 11: 1ff.). ✳

A PROPHETIC LAMENT

O sinful nation, people loaded with iniquity,   4
race of evildoers, wanton destructive children
    who have deserted the LORD,
      spurned the Holy One of Israel
      and turned your backs on him.
    Where can you still be struck   5
      if you will be disloyal still?
    Your head is covered with sores,
    your body diseased;
from head to foot there is not a sound spot in you –   6
nothing but bruises and weals and raw wounds
    which have not felt compress or bandage
    or soothing oil.
Your country is desolate, your cities lie in ashes.   7
Strangers devour your land before your eyes;
    it is desolate as Sodom[a] in its overthrow.
      Only Zion is left,   8
    like a watchman's shelter in a vineyard,
    a shed in a field of cucumbers,
      a city well guarded.
If the LORD of Hosts had not left us a remnant,   9
   we should soon have been like Sodom,
      no better than Gomorrah.

✶ Although these verses are possibly independent of verses
2–3, it is more probable that they are the prophet's application
of the divine word to the events of 701 B.C. when Judah
endured the sufferings of Sennacherib's invasion (Isa. 36);
verses 7–8 find their parallel in Sennacherib's annals: 'As for

[a] Sodom: *prob. rdg.; Heb.* strangers.

25

Hezekiah, the Jew...forty-six of his strong walled towers and innumerable smaller villages...I besieged and conquered... himself I shut up like a caged bird within Jerusalem.' The opening word of verse 4, *O*, translates the Hebrew word used in a funeral lament (cp. Jer. 22: 18). Isaiah sees the nation as virtually dead, because they have forsaken the living God. *race* might have been rendered 'family' (literally 'seed'), to preserve the progression of thought. This people is mortally ill, its country devastated, Jerusalem alone remains and it is besieged. But for this pitiful remnant, surviving by the LORD's mercy, this people would have been completely destroyed and suffered the fate of *Sodom* and *Gomorrah*. In verse 7, the Hebrew 'strangers' has been amended to *Sodom*; if the latter was original, it may have been modified from feelings of repugnance at the thought of likening the holy land to that evil city. The word for *overthrow* is only used of the destruction of Sodom and Gomorrah (cp. 13: 19 etc.). But the emphasis in this passage is not on the wickedness of those cities, but on their complete destruction. In verse 8 *a city well guarded* means that it is closely besieged by the enemy. In verse 9 the Hebrew word for *remnant* is not that used for 'remnant' elsewhere in Isaiah, and simply indicates the survivors, not the penitent and purified remnant. ✣

VAIN WORSHIP

10 Hear the word of the LORD, you rulers of Sodom;
attend, you people of Gomorrah, to the instruction of
our God:

11 Your countless sacrifices, what are they to me?
says the LORD.
I am sated with whole-offerings of rams
and the fat of buffaloes;
I have no desire for the blood of bulls,
of sheep and of he-goats.

26

Whenever you come to enter my presence[a] –   12–13
who asked you for this?
No more shall you trample my courts,
 The offer of your gifts is useless,
the reek of sacrifice is abhorrent to me.
New moons and sabbaths and assemblies,
sacred seasons and ceremonies, I cannot endure.
I cannot tolerate your new moons and your festivals;   14
 they have become a burden to me,
  and I can put up with them no longer.
  When you lift your hands outspread in prayer,   15
I will hide my eyes from you.
Though you offer countless prayers,
 I will not listen.
There is blood on your hands;
 wash yourselves and be clean.   16
Put away the evil of your deeds,
 away out of my sight.
Cease to do evil and learn to do right,   17
pursue justice and champion the oppressed;
give the orphan his rights, plead the widow's cause.

* There is no logical connection between these verses and
those in the preceding section. They could in fact have been
spoken at any period of Isaiah's ministry, probably at the
beginning. Their occurrence here provides a good illustration
of the way in which one oracle brought to mind another.
The reference to Sodom and Gomorrah in verse 9 provided
a verbal link to this oracle with its reference to those cities.
But while in verse 9 those cities are examples of total destruction, in verse 10 they are types of wickedness.

[a] *Lit.* to see my face.

Like other prophets (cp. Amos 5: 21-4; Hos. 6: 6; Mic. 6: 6-8; Jer. 7: 4-7, 21-3) Isaiah exposes the futility of ritual unless it is accompanied by righteous conduct. This is implicit throughout the law, and most eloquently in Deuteronomy, where careful attention to the ritual is closely associated with the demand for right conduct. Similarly the Psalms, and specifically those which prepare the worshipping community for entering the temple (cp. Pss. 15 and 24), require righteousness as an essential element in worship. This is what the LORD demands.

These words were probably uttered at one of the great festivals, perhaps the New Year Festival at the renewal of the covenant when the king (perhaps Ahaz), priests and representatives of the people were present. The presence of the prophet would be welcomed as one in whom the divine blessing was strong. But when the prophet spoke, his words must have come as a profound shock. They were a complete reversal of what everyone took for granted. They thought it was the function of man to provide the sacrificial food for the gods, to perform the ritual correctly and recite the ritual words. In spite of the teaching of the law, it is hardly surprising that the Israelites absorbed this point of view of the peoples of the world in which they lived. But these are not the ways for securing the blessing of the God of Israel who 'by righteousness...shows himself holy' (5: 16). Let his worshippers repent of evil conduct and practise righteousness as an essential element in their worship.

10. *instruction*: Hebrew *tōrāh*, usually translated as 'law'. The English word has too narrow a meaning for the Hebrew. Here it is parallel to the *word of the LORD*, a prophetic word. It may be understood as an authoritative instruction in answer to a question addressed to God. So *of our God* is in deliberate contrast to gods other than Israel's God. As used here it probably does not refer to a specific code of laws but to an instruction received and spoken by a true priest or prophet, perhaps in answer to a question 'What does the LORD require of us?'

28

11. *sacrifices:* a general term for animal sacrifices, in many of which the offerer shared, after the blood and the fat had been separated.

whole-offerings: those which were wholly consumed on the altar, symbolizing man's total self-committal to God.

12. *enter my presence:* a technical term for 'come to worship me'. But the literal translation 'see my face' (footnote) suggests some kind of representation of God's presence, perhaps the ark-throne.

13. *reek of sacrifice:* or, smoke of sacrifice. The word was later used of incense. In this great rejection of the worship in the temple, Isaiah is not rejecting *sacrifice* and ritual, any more than he rejects 'prayer' (15). What is condemned is worship in which ethical conduct is not included. ✲

WILL GOD FORGIVE?

Come now, let us argue it out,   18
    says the LORD.
Though your sins are scarlet,
    they may become white as snow;
    though they are dyed crimson,
    they may yet be like wool.
Obey with a will,   19
and you shall eat the best that earth yields;
    but, if you refuse and rebel,   20
    locust-beans shall be your only food.*[a]*
The LORD himself has spoken.

✲ This may be an independent oracle, and attached to the preceding oracle as developing verses 16–17. The opening words of verse 18 are in the language of the law-court: 'Plead your case.' What follows may be a promise of divine

[a] locust-beans...food: *or, with Scroll,* you shall be eaten by the sword.

forgiveness, or, it may be sarcasm: 'Can sins so heavily impregnated with crimson become white?' In the latter case verses 19-20 are in contrast; what God really looks for is obedience. It must be admitted that 19-20 is consistent with the prophetic message, while the thought of dark sins being whitened is improbable. Sins can be forgiven, removed, expiated but not made pure.

20. *locust-beans:* this rendering is justified by the similarity of the two words in Hebrew; ḥereb 'sword', ḥarub 'locust-beans'. The earlier English versions 'You shall be eaten by the sword' are hardly a translation of MT (the Hebrew text of our printed Hebrew Bibles) but are supported by the Qumran scroll of Isaiah. *

A LAMENT OVER JERUSALEM

21 How the faithful city has played the whore,
   once the home of justice where righteousness dwelt –
      but now murderers!

22   Your silver has turned into base metal
   and your liquor is diluted with water.

23   Your very rulers are rebels, confederate with thieves;
   every man of them loves a bribe
     and itches for a gift;
    they do not give the orphan his rights,
   and the widow's cause never comes before them.

* The opening words of verse 21 are in the mode of a funeral dirge, as indicated in the first word 'How' and the Hebrew metre. A similar dirge occurs in Amos 5: 2, and it is the dominant mode in Lamentations. These verses express Isaiah's own reaction to the state of Jerusalem, and lead into the divine oracle of judgement and renewal in verses 24-8.

21. *played the whore* is a metaphor not otherwise used by

Isaiah, but more characteristic of Hosea, Jeremiah and Ezekiel, where it usally refers to (a) the nation and (b) to idolatry or the worship of false gods. Here it refers more generally to Jerusalem's unfaithfulness to the righteous requirements of the divine husband; the wife has dishonoured him by her evil practices. It is to be noted that unrighteousness includes a callous disregard for the defenceless 'orphan' and 'widow' (verse 23).

23. *rulers...rebels* reproduces as well as translation can the Hebrew play on words. ✻

DIVINE JUDGEMENT AND RENEWAL

This therefore is the word of the Lord, the LORD of 24
Hosts, the Mighty One of Israel:
> Enough! I will secure a respite from my foes
> and take vengeance on my enemies.

Once again I will act against you   25
> to refine away your base metal as with potash
> and purge all your impurities;

I will again make your judges what once they were 26
> and your counsellors like those of old.

Then at length you shall be called
the home of righteousness, the faithful city.
> Justice shall redeem Zion   27
> and righteousness her repentant people.

Rebels and sinners shall be broken together 28
> and those who forsake the LORD shall cease to be.

✻ 24. The titles of God determine the character of this oracle. He is the warrior who will defend and rescue his people. But his *enemies* are now to be found within his own city. Judgement must begin with the household of God. This is one of the distinctive features of the prophetic faith. The *enemies* of God are not merely foreign nations who attack his people, but those within who by injustice are destroying and corrupting the community.

Mighty One is a rare term and it may be that Isaiah is picking up the language of Gen. 49: 24 (N.E.B. 'Strong One') and Ps. 132: 2, 5. It is a reminder of the essential unity of the twelve tribes and of the coronation prayer. The great king will rid himself of the rebels and so restore his realm to its former faithfulness.

secure a respite: an exact equivalent for the Hebrew verb is not easy to find. The metaphor is that of getting rid of a heavy burden, and the verb is variously translated 'relent' (Amos 7: 3; Ps. 106: 45); 'change his purpose' (Ps. 110: 4); 'remorsefully' (Jer. 8: 6); 'comfort' (Isa. 40: 1). Again *take vengeance on* to the modern English ear sounds vindictive. It includes restoring to his rightful position one who has been wronged, together with the punishment of the wrong-doer. So the *vengeance* in this passage includes the purification of Jerusalem as well as the destruction of those who have corrupted her life.

25. *potash* seems hardly appropriate to this smelting process, and it is possible that for *as with potash* (*kabbor*) we should read 'in the furnace' (*bakkur*) to separate the pure metal from its impurities. ✳

AN END TO PAGAN WORSHIP

29 For the sacred oaks in which you delighted shall fail you,[a]

the garden-shrines of your fancy shall disappoint you.

30 You shall be like a terebinth whose leaves have withered, like a garden without water;

31 the strongest tree[b] shall become like tow,

[a] *So some MSS.: others* them. [b] *Or* the strong man.

and what is made of it*a* shall go up in sparks,
and the two shall burst into flames together
with no one to quench them.

✵ The introductory word 'For' suggests that this oracle is
the concluding judgement of the 'rebels' and 'sinners' of
the preceding verses. Yet the contents of this oracle are
concerned with the worship of nature-deities rather than with
injustice. This oracle may be compared with 17: 10–11 and
Hos. 4: 13, the latter passage being specifically addressed
to the northern kingdom. During the reign of Ahaz, there
was a reversion to the Canaanite worship of nature deities,
referred to in generalized terms in 2 Kings 16: 4. The oracle
may have been addressed to Judah during the reign of Ahaz,
but the resemblance to Hos. 4: 13 suggests the possibility that
it was addressed to Israel.

29. The *sacred oaks* and *garden-shrines* were regular places
of fertility cults, and often associated with orgiastic rites (Jer.
3: 6, 9). Isaiah saw this kind of religion as not only futile, but
destructive since it was a departure from the covenant-
relationship with God. ✵

UNIVERSAL PEACE UNDER GOD'S RULE

This is the word which Isaiah son of Amoz received in **2**
a vision concerning Judah and Jerusalem.

In days to come   2*b*
the mountain of the LORD's house
shall be set over all other mountains,
lifted high above the hills.
All the nations shall come streaming to it,
and many peoples shall come and say,   **3**

[a] *Or* what he makes.   [b] *Verses 2–4: cp. Mic. 4: 1–3.*

'Come, let us climb up on to the mountain of the LORD,
    to the house of the God of Jacob,
      that he may teach us his ways
      and we may walk in his paths.'
    For instruction issues from Zion,
      and out of Jerusalem comes the word of the LORD;
4   he will be judge between nations,
    arbiter among many peoples.
    They shall beat their swords into mattocks
      and their spears into pruning-knives;[a]
  nation shall not lift sword against nation
    nor ever again be trained for war.

5   O people of Jacob, come,
    let us walk in the light of the LORD.

＊ The superscription in verse 1 makes it evident that we have here a collection of Isaiah's oracles which is independent of ch. 1. This collection appears to have been concluded with the oracles in 4: 2-6. Thus we have a series of judgement oracles contained in a frame of hope for the future (2: 2-5; 4: 2-6). The judgement oracles may best be associated with the early ministry of Isaiah. Less certainty attaches to the opening and closing words of hope.

The poem, verses 2-4, occurs again with slight variations in Mic. 4: 1-3 with an extra verse (Mic. 4: 4), and the comment Isa. 2: 5 is similar to Mic. 4: 5, although fuller in Micah. In form it is a hymn of the temple and may have belonged to a collection of such hymns before being included in the collections of Isaiah's and Micah's prophecies. Most commentators regard the poem as post-exilic, but the arguments for doing so are not conclusive. The inclusion of this poem, presumably by the disciples of Isaiah, to precede the terrifying description

[a] They shall beat...pruning-knives: *cp. Joel* 3: 9-12.

of the day of the Lord and looking beyond that to the fulfilment of his purpose for his people, is singularly appropriate.
Judgement is not completed in punishment, but in forgiveness
and purification.

A remarkable feature of this poem is not only its universalism, but its freedom from narrow nationalism. It is true
that it speaks of Jerusalem and the temple. But Jerusalem is
not merely David's royal city, nor is it seen as an impregnable
fortress. It is exalted but open to all, when the nations may
learn the way of life, to which they may come to find settlement of their disputes and in which they may transform
weapons of war into tools of production. This may well be the
fulfilment of the ancient covenant-promise that Israel will
be the LORD's kingdom of priests, keeping and teaching the
divine instruction for all mankind (Exod. 19: 5–6). The nations
of the world come not to conquer (Ps. 2: 1–3), nor as subdued
and crushed (Pss. 46, 48, 76) but to hear 'the word of the
LORD'.

2. *In days to come:* originally a term to indicate the remote
future (Gen. 49: 1; Num. 24: 14), but used especially by the
prophets to indicate the fulfilment of God's rule (cp. Hos. 3:
5). It is that future which, in the prophetic teaching, determines action in the present. Amidst all the confusions and
uncertainties of the present, the prophet sees that goal in
human history which is certain and inevitable because it is
the divinely appointed goal. It is this which gives meaning to
the present, and furnishes a basis for judgement on men's
actions. All history, past, present and future, is held in a unity,
the unity of the divine rule. Other phrases associated with
this are 'in that day', 'in those days', 'the day of the Lord'.
A term that has been used in this connection is 'realized
eschatology', but this can be misleading. The End, as goal, is
not merely 'realized' by the prophet, it *is* present, because
the 'now' and the 'End' are indissolubly linked in the purpose
of God into which the prophet has been drawn. It may be
thought of in terms of the drama, where it is the end which

determines the actions of the characters, whether they know it or not, in all the acts of the play.

4. *They shall beat...* is reversed in Joel 3: 10.

5. N.E.B. makes this introductory to 6–22, but it is better to regard this as the prophet's word to the congregation. The *people of Jacob* have received the revelation and it is their role in history to *walk in the light* in order that 'all the nations' may learn 'his ways'. ✲

THE GREAT DAY OF THE LORD

6   Thou hast abandoned thy people the house of Jacob;
       for they are crowded with traders[a]
       and barbarians like the Philistines,
       and with the children of foreigners everywhere.

7   Their land is filled with silver and gold,
         and there is no end to their treasure;
       their land is filled with horses,
         and there is no end to their chariots;

8   their land is filled with idols,
       and they bow down to the work of their own hands,
       to what their fingers have made.

9   Mankind shall be brought low,
       all men shall be humbled;
       and how can they raise themselves?[b]

10   Get you into the rocks and hide yourselves in the ground
      from the dread of the LORD and the splendour of his majesty.

[a] *Or* hawkers.   [b] *Prob. rdg.; Heb.* and do not forgive them.

Man's proud eyes shall be humbled,   11
   the loftiness of men brought low,
and the LORD alone shall be exalted
   on that day.

For the LORD of Hosts has a day of doom waiting   12
   for all that is proud and lofty,
   for all that is high*a* and lifted up,
for all the cedars of Lebanon, lofty and high,   13
   and for all the oaks of Bashan,
for all lofty mountains and for all high hills,   14
for every high tower and for every sheer wall,   15
for all ships of Tarshish and all the dhows of Arabia.*b* 16
   Then man's pride shall be brought low,   17
   and the loftiness of man shall be humbled,
and the LORD alone shall be exalted
   on that day,
  while the idols shall pass away utterly.   18
Get you into caves in the rocks   19
   and crevices in the ground
from the dread of the LORD and the splendour of his
     majesty,
  when he rises to inspire the earth with fear.
On that day a man shall fling away   20
his idols of silver and his idols of gold
  which he has made for himself to worship;
he shall fling them to the dung-beetles and the bats,
and creep into clefts in the rocks and crannies in the   21
     cliffs

[*a*] *So Sept.; Heb.* low.
[*b*] the dhows of Arabia: *mng. of Heb. words uncertain.*

from the dread of the LORD and the splendour of his
  majesty,
 when he rises to inspire the earth with fear.
22 Have no more to do with man, for what is he worth?
 He is no more than the breath in his nostrils.

* In powerful contrast to the mood of the preceding hymn,
this passage describes what the Day will mean for those who
replace total dependence on God with reliance on wealth,
military strength and pagan religion. These, 'the work of
their own hands', only foster human pride, and blind men's
eyes to the reality which is the active rule of God. Here the
prophet is himself giving his assessment of his people's condition. This section can confidently be associated with the
earliest period of the prophetic ministry, before the advance
of the Assyrian armies or even the attack on the kingdom led
by Rezin and Pekah (ch. 7) had drained away its wealth.

This section contains two sets of repeated refrains though
with some variations: (A) 10, 19, 21; (B) 11, 17 and possibly 9.
In (A) the first two are imperatives and the third is in Hebrew
an infinitive (i.e. 'to creep') while in (B) 9 appears to be a
modification of 11 and 17. These variations would be surprising, unless they were original, since one would expect a
later collector to make them all the same. It is possible that
the prophetic words with refrains were uttered on different
occasions and have been gathered together in this section
because of the obvious similarity of themes, and especially
the threefold reference to idols (8, 18, 20). A somewhat
similar verse to the B refrains appears in 5: 15 in a prophetic
speech which might support the idea of a variety of occasions.
Variations within a refrain occur also in Pss. 80 and 107 and
may well be a skilful way of emphasizing the main theme by
introducing a new element.

6. *traders:* this interprets a word which means 'from the
east', which most understand, by emending a letter, as

'diviners' (so the Revised Standard Version); *barbarians:* the Hebrew word is usually understood to mean 'diviners' as in Jer. 29: 9. The verse then refers either to commercial undertakings (N.E.B.) or to the practice of sorcery. The reference to the *house of Jacob* suggests that Isaiah was including the northern kingdom in his denunciation.

8. *idols,* i.e. worthless things (cp. 18, 20). The Hebrew word *'elilim* is a scornful pun on *'elim,* gods. The word *'elilim* is not found in writings earlier than this passage in Isaiah. It is, however, used in Lev. 19: 4; 26: 1, and there is reason to believe that much of the contents of Lev. 17–26 (the holiness code) derives from the teaching of the Jerusalem priests. If the word was used in temple teaching in Isaiah's day, the prophet was making skilful use of the word because it was well known.

9. *how can they raise themselves?* the footnote 'do not forgive them' is closer to the Hebrew, but the line is obscure, and lacking in the Qumran scroll.

10. The limestone rocks of Palestine provided many caves in which, during invasion, fugitives could take refuge, as they did during the Maccabean revolt and the Roman wars. *Dread of the LORD:* cp. 19 and 21. This is the mysterious fear induced by God, and is first used in 1 Sam. 11: 7. In Gen. 31: 42, 53, the word Dread (Fear) is used as a proper name for the God of Isaac. In Hab. 2: 20 and Zech. 2: 13 this dread in the divine presence produces an awed silence. *splendour of his majesty* is a phrase peculiar to these refrains and recalls Isaiah's own vision of God in ch. 6.

16. *ships of Tarshish:* vessels used originally by the Phoenicians to carry cargo from their copper refineries, and so by Solomon in connection with his smelting plant near Eziongeber (1 Kings 10: 22), possibly discovered by archaeologists. The brief reference to the restoration of Elath in 2 Kings 14: 22 may indicate that Uzziah (Azariah) was able for a while to regain this area and the wealth from its copper. *dhows of Arabia:* a probably correct rendering of an obscure phrase of

which the first word certainly means some kind of ship. Other renderings are 'beautiful vessels' or 'vessels bearing luxury cargoes'.

20. *dung-beetles:* this replaces 'moles' in earlier versions. The Hebrew word must mean a digging creature, but moles do not inhabit rocky places. This beetle gathers animal droppings as food, rolls the dung into a ball and carries it into a crevice. Known as the scarab, it was venerated in Egypt.

22. This verse is regarded as a later comment on the preceding poem. But who are being addressed? The first verb is plural. A similar sentiment occurs in Ps. 146: 3–4 with the first verb also in the plural. The verse in Isaiah may then be the comment to the worshipping community after reading this poem. Since the verse does not occur in the Septuagint it is probably quite late. ✳

ANARCHY

3 Be warned: the Lord, the LORD of Hosts,
    is stripping Jerusalem and Judah
        of every prop and stay,[a]
2   warrior and soldier,
    judge and prophet, diviner and elder,
3   captains of companies[b] and men of rank,
        counsellor, magician, and cunning enchanter.
4   Then I will appoint mere boys to be their captains,
        who shall govern as the fancy takes them;
5   the people shall deal harshly
    each man with his fellow and with his neighbour;
        children shall break out against their elders,
            and nobodies against men of substance.

[a] *Prob. rdg.; Heb. adds* all stay of bread and all stay of water.
[b] companies: *lit.* units of fifty.

If a man takes hold of his brother in his father's house, 6
saying, 'You have a cloak, you shall be our chief;
   our stricken family shall be under you',
he will cry out that day and say, 7
     'I will not be your master;
   there is neither bread nor cloak in my house,
   and you shall not make me head of the clan.'
Jerusalem is stricken and Judah fallen 8
   because they have spoken and acted against the LORD,
     rebelling against the glance of his glorious eye.
   The look on their faces testifies against them; 9
   like Sodom they proclaim their sins
     and do not conceal them.[a]
Woe upon them! they have earned their own disaster.
   Happy[b] the righteous man! all goes well with 10
     him,
   for such men enjoy the fruit of their actions.
   Woe betide the wicked! with him all goes ill, 11
   for he reaps the reward that he has earned.
   Money-lenders strip my people bare, 12
   and usurers lord it over them.
   O my people! your guides lead you astray
     and confuse the path that you should take.
   The LORD comes forward to argue his case 13
   and stands to judge his people.[c]
   The LORD opens the indictment 14
   against the elders of his people and their officers:
   You have ravaged the vineyard,

[a] like...them: *or* and their sins, like those of Sodom, denounce them;
they do not deny them.   [b] *Prob. rdg.; Heb.* Say.
[c] his people: *so Sept.; Heb.* peoples.

and the spoils of the poor are in your houses.
15   Is it nothing to you that you crush my people
            and grind the faces of the poor?
This is the very word of the Lord, the LORD of Hosts.

✻ This section may be subdivided: (A) 1-9, the breakdown of
society; (B) 10-11, a wisdom saying; (C) 12-15, the government is judged. The sayings are not dated, but the contents, at
least of (A) and (C), would fit well into what we know of the
early years of the reign of Ahaz. Isaiah describes a society
whose leaders have betrayed their trust. It is because the
prophet held an exalted conception of government, that he
denounces so fiercely the abuse of power by those who
should lead the Lord's people in ways of healthy mutual trust
and prosperity. The danger is that misgovernment may breed
violence and a situation in which upstarts may seize power.
In these years there was a growing fearfulness at the approach
of the Assyrian armies, and this bred a determination to get
what one could for oneself while there was time. When once
lawlessness and violence has broken out, little short of a
miracle can restore law and order.

1-9. The breakdown of society.

1. *the Lord:* this title is characteristic of Isaiah's oracles.
It is not the same as the following *the LORD* which represents
the divine name Yahweh, and indicates God's sovereignty.
It is probably a title used in the temple liturgies and associated
with covenant celebration (cp. Exod. 23: 17; 34: 23). The
prophet deliberately uses this title in threatening oracles (1: 24;
10: 16, 33; 19: 4) as if to overturn the false confidence arising
from its ritual use. The succeeding title, *the LORD of Hosts*
(*Yahweh tseba'oth*), further emphasizes the divine omnipotence
in contrast to the weakness of Judah's *every prop and stay*.
(The phrase in N.E.B. footnote, 'all stay of bread and all
stay of water' was apparently either a deliberate reapplication
of this oracle to the siege of 587 or a marginal note in the

Hebrew manuscript made by a teacher who remembered
Ezek. 4: 16, and later brought into the text).

2-7. The list follows of those responsible for the welfare
of society. The presence of diviners, magicians and *cunning*
(i.e. skilful) enchanters would be normal in the ancient Near
East, although they were rejected in Israel's law. Among them
also were such prophets as we meet in 1 Kings 22: 6ff.; cp.
Mic. 3: 6, 7, 11. Surprisingly no reference is made in this list
to the king and the priest. The background of this oracle
would suggest the early years of the reign of King Ahaz
who came to the throne at the age of twenty (2 Kings 16: 2)
when Judah was attacked by the forces of Israel and Syria
(2 Kings 16: 5; Isa. 7: 1-6). The removal of the experienced
leaders meant that the conduct of affairs had been seized by
untrained and incompetent upstarts (4f.), resulting in chaos.
Finally, none would accept responsibility for leadership (6f.).
Isaiah finds the real cause of this social breakdown in rebellion
against God.

10-11. This wisdom saying, whose style resembles that of
Proverbs, may have been added later by a commentator,
but it may be a quotation by Isaiah (or his disciples) from
contemporary wisdom. From the time of Solomon something
like a guild of wise men had become part of the court personnel. Similar passages occur elsewhere in Isaiah (cp. 32: 5-8).

12-15. Judgement. The court-scene of this oracle is more
than a figure of speech. God *is* the great king and after the
manner of kings summons the leaders of his people to account
for their misrule. But the repeated *my people* relates this
to the covenant which they have violated. In fact they have
behaved like those from whom God rescued them in Egypt
(Exod. 3: 7f.), or like the Philistine oppressors and they can expect the same punishment. It is probable that verses 12, 14*b*-15
are the words of God uttered directly through the prophet,
while verses 13-14*a* represent the prophet's description of
what he sees in prophetic vision.

14. *You have ravaged the vineyard:* the phrase probably

points to the specific occasion of the oracle, the Autumn
Festival when the covenant was celebrated, and the active
rule of God was acknowledged. Doubtless Isaiah refers
specifically to burdensome taxes imposed on the cultivation,
but at a deeper level he refers to the way in which the leaders
have ill-treated God's vineyard. (The Septuagint has 'my
vineyard', that is the people of God whom it is the leaders'
responsibility to protect and maintain.) The vineyard theme
is developed in Isa. 5: 1-7; cp. Isa. 27: 2; Jer. 2: 21; 5: 10;
12: 10. ✻

THE FASHIONABLE LADIES OF JERUSALEM

16   Then the LORD said:
Because the women of Zion hold themselves high
and walk with necks outstretched and wanton glances,
    moving with mincing gait
    and jingling feet,
17 the Lord will give the women of Zion bald heads,
the LORD will strip the hair from their foreheads.

18   In that day the Lord will take away all finery: anklets,
19, 20 discs, crescents, pendants, bangles, coronets, head-bands,
21 armlets, necklaces, lockets, charms, signets, nose-rings,
22, 23 fine dresses, mantles, cloaks, flounced skirts, scarves of
gauze, kerchiefs of linen, turbans, and flowing veils.

24   So instead of perfume you shall have the stench of decay,
        and a rope in place of a girdle,
    baldness instead of hair elegantly coiled,
    a loin-cloth of sacking instead of a mantle,
    and branding instead of beauty.
25   Your men shall fall by the sword,
    and your warriors in battle;

then Zion's gates shall mourn and lament,   26
    and she shall sit on the ground stripped bare.

  Then on that day   **4**
seven women shall take hold of one man and say,
  'We will eat our own bread and wear our own clothes
    if only we may be called by your name;
      take away our disgrace.'

* Like other prophets (cp. Amos 4: 1), Isaiah recognizes that
the women who use their husbands' wealth, gained by extortion, to squander on senseless luxury, are also to blame. Their
doom is certain. The section could be sub-divided: 3: 16–24
(the detailed list of feminine adornments was probably added
to the oracle, perhaps by a disciple of the prophet) in which
the luxurious dress is exchanged for that of captive women;
and 3: 25 – 4: 1 which describes the effect of the war. Men
had been killed in battle, many others taken prisoner and en-
slaved. So many women would be left defenceless and child-
less, a condition regarded as shameful in the oriental world.

  25. *Your* is now singular; the prophet turns from the
women to the mother, i.e. Zion, to announce the doom on
the city as she mourns the loss of her warriors. *

A PROMISE OF RESTORATION

  On that day the plant that the LORD has grown   2
    shall become glorious in its beauty,
  and the fruit of the land shall be
      the pride and splendour
      of the survivors of Israel.

  Then those who are left in Zion, who remain in Jeru-   3
salem, every one enrolled in the book of life,[a] shall be
called holy. If the Lord washes away the filth of the   4

[a] enrolled...life: *lit.* written for life.

women of Zion and cleanses Jerusalem from the blood
that is in it by a spirit of judgement, a consuming spirit,
5 then over every building on Mount Zion and on all her
places of assembly the LORD will create a cloud of smoke
by day and a bright flame of fire by night; for glory shall
6 be spread over all as a covering and a canopy, a shade from
the heat by day, a refuge and a shelter from rain and tempest.

✶ Of these verses, 2 may be in poetic form, as suggested by
the N.E.B., but the remainder are prose. It is possible that
verse 2 is an oracle of Isaiah, but 3–6 belongs to a later age.
They appear to be the reflection on an oracle of Isaiah, but
applied to the circumstances of a later age. The phrases *book
of life*, *cloud of smoke by day* and *fire by night* derive from liturgical usage (cp. Exod. 32: 32; 13: 21f.; 40: 34–8), although
the latter phrases are used here to denote protection rather
than the guiding Presence. The passage as a whole refers to
those who return from exile to take up again the ancient role
of the people of God in the new age. ✶

THE PARABLE OF THE VINEYARD

5   I will sing for my beloved
      my love-song about his vineyard:
    My beloved had a vineyard
      high up on a fertile hill-side.
2   He trenched it and cleared it of stones
      and planted it with red vines;
    he built a watch-tower in the middle
    and then hewed out a winepress in it.
    He looked for it to yield grapes,
      but it yielded wild grapes.

Now, you who live in Jerusalem,   3
   and you men of Judah,
judge between me and my vineyard.
What more could have been done for my vineyard   4
that I did not do in it?
Why, when I looked for it to yield grapes,
   did it yield wild grapes?
Now listen while I tell you   5
what I will do to my vineyard:
I will take away its fences and let it be burnt,
I will break down its walls and let it be trampled
   underfoot,
   and so I will leave it derelict;   6
it shall be neither pruned nor hoed,
but shall grow thorns and briars.
   Then I will command the clouds
to send no more rain upon it.
The vineyard of the LORD of Hosts is Israel,   7
   and the men of Judah are the plant he cherished.
He looked for justice and found it denied,
   for righteousness but heard cries of distress.

✳ This is one of the finest and most powerful examples of a
form of teaching of which many occurrences appear in the
Old Testament and in the teaching of Jesus. Its function is to
engage the attention of the hearers, to invite a judgement on
the situation described in the parable; they may then see
that that judgement is in fact on themselves and their conduct,
and this may lead to repentance. Sometimes, as here, the
point is made explicit by the prophet; sometimes the similarity
is left to those who have 'ears to hear'.
The skill with which this parable is presented may be seen

in that it begins with words associated with love-songs. In the ears of the hearers this would be particularly appropriate at the vintage season, since they would immediately connect the 'song' with the fertility myths of the ancient world, celebrating the union of the male and female deities. But this quickly (verse 3) becomes a trial, in which the hearers are invited to pass a judgement. The inevitable penalty is then declared by the prophet (verses 5–6), the justice of which would be acknowledged as fully appropriate. Then comes the point of the parable: you are the worthless vineyard! (verse 7). We may compare Nathan's parable in 2 Sam. 12: 1–7.

1. Although some have interpreted *my beloved* as referring to God, this is both unnecessary and improbable. The song is not an allegory in which one has to find an equivalent for each expression. It is most improbable that Isaiah would equate the Hebrew word for *beloved*, which has close connections with fertility myths, as a title for Israel's God. But to many of his hearers this kind of equation would be appropriate, since in popular religion the god was the husband (lover) of the land. Their union ensured the fertility of the soil. Nothing of this appears in the song.

2. Rather does the 'beloved' patiently work to clear the vineyard and protect it. Having planted in it the best kind of grape-vine, he had every reason to expect a good crop. But the incredible happened. The crop was not merely poor in quantity; that would have suggested inadequate cultivation. It was of bitter *wild grapes*, useless and offensive. The English equivalent would be an orchard planted with Blenheim Orange apples that produced crab-apples! There is only one thing to be done with a vineyard that behaves in such an unnatural way – abandon it. Everyone would agree.

7. Then comes the final sentence. 'You are that vineyard!' The closing sentence is the more effective in Hebrew because it includes a powerful play on words which can hardly be reproduced in another language: *justice (mishpāṭ)...denied*

(*mispāḥ*), *righteousness* (*tsedāqāh*)...cries of *distress* (*tseʿāqāh*).
An attempt to convey this might be to say:

'He looked for the light of justice and found the night of
bloodshed,

for compassion and found oppression.' ✶

SHAME ON YOU!

Shame on you! you who add house to house   8
and join field to field,
until not an acre remains,
and you are left to dwell alone in the land.
The LORD of Hosts has sworn[a] in my hearing: 9
Many houses shall go to ruin,
fine large houses shall be uninhabited.
Five acres[b] of vineyard shall yield only a gallon,[c]   10
and ten bushels[d] of seed return only a peck.[e]
Shame on you! you who rise early in the morning   11
to go in pursuit of liquor
and draw out the evening inflamed with wine,
at whose feasts there are harp and lute,   12
tabor and pipe and wine,
who have no eyes for the work of the LORD,
and never see the things that he has done.
Therefore my people are dwindling away   13
all unawares;
the nobles are starving to death,
and the common folk die of thirst.
Therefore Sheol gapes with straining throat   14
and has opened her measureless jaws:

[a] has sworn: *prob. rdg.; Heb. om.* [b] *Lit.* Ten yokes. [c] *Heb.* bath.
[d] *Heb.* homer. [e] *Heb.* ephah.

down go nobility and common people,
　　their noisy bustling mob.*a*

15　Mankind is brought low, men are humbled,
　　　humbled are haughty looks.

16　But the LORD of Hosts sits high in judgement,
　　and by righteousness the holy God shows himself holy.

17　Young rams shall feed where fat bullocks once pastured,
　　and kids shall graze broad acres where cattle grew fat.*b*

18　Shame on you! you who drag wickedness along like a
　　　tethered sheep
　　and sin like a heifer on a rope,

19　who say, 'Let the LORD*c* make haste,
　　let him speed up his work for us to see it,
　　let the purpose of the Holy One of Israel
　　be soon fulfilled, so that we may know it.'

20　Shame on you! you who call evil good and good evil,
　　who turn darkness into light and light into darkness,
　　who make bitter sweet and sweet bitter.

21　Shame on you! you who are wise in your own eyes
　　　and prudent in your own esteem.

22　Shame on you! you mighty topers, valiant mixers of
　　　drink,

23　who for a bribe acquit the guilty
　　and deny justice to those in the right.

✻ There are six or perhaps seven oracles in this section, and
a further oracle of a similar character in 10: 1–4. They were
normally introduced by the exclamation 'Shame on you'
which may also have introduced a clause before 14. The

[*a*] nobility...mob; *or* nobility, common people and noisy mob, and
are restless there.　[*b*] Young...grew fat: *prob. rdg.; Heb. unintelligible.*
[*c*] the LORD: *so Pesh.; Heb. om.*

exclamation is properly a cry of grief and is translated by 'O' in 1: 4 and 'Listen!' in 17: 12. Although, as in this section, it may be followed by a rebuke, that rebuke is uttered with grief. Those who are addressed suppose themselves to be in a state of security and prosperity, but they are in fact on the brink of disaster. By their conduct they have cut themselves off from the living God, the source of life, so that the prophet laments over them as though they were dead. The lament by implication prepares the way for a divine judgement. That judgement is explicit at the end of the first two oracles (9f., 13), and may originally have followed the others. The whole section probably comes from the earliest period of Isaiah's ministry.

8–10. The landgrabbers. In the towns of Palestine, houses were built close together, rich and poor living cheek by jowl. As merchants grew rich through their commercial undertakings, they sought to buy up houses in the city and the peasant holdings in the country. So the poor became homeless and without land for the growing of food. But this left the peasant no alternative but to sell himself into slavery. This was not only inhumane, but a defiance of Israel's faith that God was the owner of the land and that he had apportioned it to each Israelite family (cp. Lev. 25: 23). Other prophets had denounced this landgrabbing, cp. 1 Kings 21; Mic. 2: 2, 9. It was seen as a destruction of the covenant-society. The divine judgement is that the land will revert to jungle. In human terms, those who have devoted their life to commerce are ill-equipped for farming, which requires a highly specialized skill based on experience. Moreover, in those days a house in the open country was inviting attack from raiders.

11–13. Compare 28: 1–13. The picture of men drunk from early morning to late at night may be deliberate exaggeration, but the point is clear. Their critical faculties are dulled. Intent upon their selfish pleasure, they are unable to discern the meaning of Israel's existence, or the significance of the events of their day. They could not discern, perhaps did not wish to discern, the activity of God. It may well be more comfortable not to do so, but it is disastrous.

13. *dwindling away:* the Hebrew verb usually means 'go into exile'. The word is not otherwise used in this sense by Isaiah, and if this oracle is early, the thought of exile may be thought inappropriate (hence this translation). But the international scene made exile a real possibility.

all unawares may mean 'unaware of God' as in Hos. 4: 1, 6, that is, lacking that awareness of the divine purpose that is born of fellowship with God.

Verse 14 is not a continuation of verse 13, but a new judgement. It may have been preceded by a 'Shame on you' clause which has now been lost.

Sheol, the underworld of the dead, is portrayed as the great monster of the ancient Semitic myth seeking to engulf the whole created world.

15. A fragment; cp. 2: 9, 11, 17.

16. Although not obviously connected with what precedes, this verse contains one of the great words of Isaiah. Holiness is a term in general use in the Semitic world but without any necessary moral content. To say that God is holy is to say that he is mysterious and unapproachable by man except through the appointed rituals. But here the great affirmation is made that the essence of the divine is *righteousness*. This distinguishes Israel's religion from that of its contemporaries. The divine sovereignty is ethically conditioned; *righteousness* is exalted to the highest place in the universe. This lies at the heart of Isaiah's understanding of history. This is of course implicit in Israel's religion from the beginning. It becomes explicit in this prophet's teaching.

17. May be the original conclusion of verse 14, but the Hebrew text makes any translation tentative (see footnote). It could mean that when the city and its inhabitants have disappeared (verse 14), sheep and goats will graze among the ruins.

18–19. The scoffers who do not share Isaiah's faith in God,

the ruler of history – and this is at the heart of Israel's religion – make life harder for themselves. It is as though they were all the time dragging a struggling sheep or heifer! They scoff at the thought that God can or will do anything effective. After all, the gods of Canaan (popular religion) were not thought of in this way, why should they suppose that Yahweh will? Yet in turning away from (the word for *sin* has this meaning) him who released them from the burden of oppression, they make life burdensome.

20. The cynics. In a polytheistic religion such as that of Canaan this inability to recognize any absolute moral standards is all too possible. There was in fact a wisdom saying current in the Semitic world which said, 'What is good in the sight of one god is evil in the sight of another.' In departing from Yahweh who had 'told you what is good' (Mic. 6: 8) men were left in this moral confusion. Amos referred to fornication practised in the name of religion (Amos 2: 7). Canaanite religion required this! Ahaz sacrificed his son as a burnt-offering (2 Kings 16: 3), a practice approved, although only as an extreme measure, by the religion of Canaan! But Israel is without excuse, for she has received the light to guide her in the way, and the divine instruction that is sweeter than honey (Ps. 19: 8–10).

21. Those who are wise in their own eyes. The specific reference is to the political advisers of the king. These were the wise men who in the light of the 'wisdom' of past experience gave guidance on public affairs, and especially in matters of foreign alliances. What prophets like Isaiah had to say about reliance on God was all very well for the sanctuary, but they were practical men. In other words, religion and politics don't mix; popular religion would support them.

22–3. Drunken judges. Some would treat these verses as two separate oracles of which the *Shame on you!* of the second has been omitted. In that case verse 22 will refer to the royal body-guard (*mighty* and *valiant* are both nouns in Hebrew and often refer to warriors) who are boastful when drunk but fearful when sober. Then verse 23 would refer to the all-too-common perversions of justice which the prophets condemn. For justice, as they saw it, was not abstract justice, not even what was embodied in the law of the land. It is the covenant law of the divine king, of which the Davidic king was the divinely appointed guardian (cp. Ps. 72: 1f.).

These verses may, however, be taken together, as in the N.E.B. Obviously fuddled minds are ill-equipped to discern the truth of a case before them, and are disposed to give judgement in favour of their host of the night before. There may be a further point. Many Israelites still thought of wine as the gift of the fertility deities (cp. Hos. 2: 5, 8). To get drunk was a way of being filled with the god. Justice was no concern of these Canaanite deities, but from the beginning Yahweh was known as the righteous judge. He demands that men act justly. (It should be noted that some would see 5: 24, which the N.E.B. gives to follow 10: 4, as the proper judgement-word to follow 5: 23.) ✳

IMMINENT DISASTER

26[a]   So he will hoist a signal to a nation far away,
      he will whistle to call them from the end of the earth;
        and see, they come, speedy and swift;

27   none is weary, not one of them stumbles,
        not one slumbers or sleeps.
      None has his belt loose about his waist
        or a broken thong to his sandals.

28   Their arrows are sharpened and their bows all strung,
      their horses' hooves flash like shooting stars,
        their chariot-wheels are like the whirlwind.

29   Their growling is the growling of a lioness,
      they growl like young lions,

[a] *Verses 24 and 25 transposed to follow 10: 4.*

which roar as they seize the prey
  and carry it beyond reach of rescue.
They shall roar over it on that day   30
  like the roaring of the sea.
If a man looks over the earth, behold, darkness closing
    in,
  and the light darkened on the hill-tops[a] !

✳ Some would associate these verses with 9: 8 – 10: 4 but
there is no unanimity about the precise point at which in that
section these verses should come. We may follow the N.E.B.
and see them as a fitting conclusion to a series of utterances
that have rebuked a society corrupted by its various leaders.
They may have been originally addressed to the northern
kingdom at the incidence of the Assyrian invasion (cp. 10:
5ff.) and later applied to Judah. In any case the argument is
clear. The Assyrian armies are coming not merely in the
interests of imperial expansion, but because God has summoned
them against his own people who, by their ill-conduct, have
broken the covenant relationship.

27–30. This vividly describes the enemy army in battle
array. The noise of their advance is like that of a lion about to
leap on its prey, or like the noise of a great tidal wave threatening to overwhelm the land. The final sentence presents the
picture of that terrible chaos when darkness covered the earth
before the work of creation (cp. also 8: 22). The disorder in
the divinely created society has affected the whole creation,
bringing chaos into the divine order of the world. ✳

[a] hill-tops: *or* clouds.

The call of Isaiah

6 IN THE YEAR of King Uzziah's death I saw the Lord
seated on a throne, high and exalted, and the skirt of
2 his robe filled the temple. About him were attendant
seraphim, and each had six wings; one pair covered his
face and one pair his feet, and one pair was spread in
3 flight. They were calling ceaselessly to one another,

> Holy, holy, holy is the LORD of Hosts:
> the whole earth is full of his glory.

4 And, as each one called, the threshold shook to its founda-
5 tions, while the house was filled with smoke. Then I cried,

> Woe is me! I am lost,
> for I am a man of unclean lips
> and I dwell among a people of unclean lips;
> yet with these eyes I have seen the King, the LORD of
> Hosts.

6 Then one of the seraphim flew to me carrying in his hand
a glowing coal which he had taken from the altar with a
7 pair of tongs. He touched my mouth with it and said,

> See, this has touched your lips;
> your iniquity is removed,
> and your sin is wiped away.

8 Then I heard the Lord saying, Whom shall I send? Who
will go for me? And I answered, Here am I: send me.
9 He said, Go and tell this people:

You may listen and listen, but you will not understand.*a*
You may look and look again, but you will never
   know.*b*
This people's wits are dulled,   10
their ears are deafened and their eyes blinded,
   so that they cannot see with their eyes
   nor listen with their ears
   nor understand with their wits,
so that they may turn and be healed.

Then I asked, How long, O Lord? And he answered,   11

Until cities fall in ruins and are deserted,
   houses are left without people,
and the land goes to ruin and lies waste,
   until the LORD has sent all mankind far away,   12
   and the whole country is one vast desolation.
   Even if a tenth part of its people remain there,   13
   they too will be exterminated
      [like an oak or a terebinth,
   a sacred pole thrown out from its place in a hill-
      shrine*c*].

٭ While other prophets have left an account of their call to
prophecy (Amos 7: 15; Jer. 1: 4–10; Ezek. 1 – 3: 15) this is
remarkable for its dramatic and majestic quality. It was, of
course, a visionary experience, but one that was initiated by
the events taking place in the temple. While Isaiah does not
state that he was in the Jerusalem temple, the various elements
of the vision can be best understood as a transforming of what

[a] *Or* but how will you understand?   [b] *Or* but how will you know?
[c] a sacred pole...hill-shrine: *prob. rdg.; Heb. obscure.*

57

was taking place during some celebration of God's rule (cp. Pss. 97–9). It is as though everything the prophet could see or hear in common with others present became the vehicle for the vision of God enthroned in his heavenly palace/temple (the Hebrew word could mean both). Whether 'the year of King Uzziah's death' (about 742 B.C.) is any more than a convenient way of fixing the date, is disputed. There is, however, a similar note in 14: 28 and what follows in verse 29 suggests what commonly happened at the death of a king, a period of confusion and rebellion of subject territories. Since Uzziah according to 2 Chron. 26 was a successful king and had re-established Solomon's refinery near Ezion-geber, as well as subduing the Philistines, his death might well have been the signal for revolt (cp. also Ps. 2: 1–3). This provides an effective contrast to the words that follow; the sovereign Lord rules from his exalted throne, whether earthly kings live or die. Yet the disorders which would follow upon the death of a successful king, would also stimulate the prophet's concern with international affairs which is so apparent in Isaiah's career. However far from popular expectations Isaiah's words were, it was the recognized function of a prophet that he should speak a 'word of the Lord' at a time of national crisis (cp. especially 1 Kings 22: 1–28).

2. *seraphim:* just as an earthly king has his attendant council, so the Lord is accompanied by superhuman beings (cp. 1 Kings 22: 19). The designation *seraphim* (Hebrew plural of *saraph*) here and in verse 6 is peculiar to Isaiah, but the word occurs also at 14: 29; 30: 6; Num. 21: 6, 8 ('serpent') and Deut. 8: 15 ('snakes'). The word means 'burning ones' and may be associated with the appearance of lightning. The visionary experience may have been stimulated by the bronze serpent in the temple (2 Kings 18: 4) although a different Hebrew word is used. The *seraphim* are depicted as having a serpent body, wings, and human head and hands. The total effect is to convey the sense of awe in the presence of the majesty of God, before whom even such 'unearthly' beings

veil themselves. This is further expressed in the continuous antiphonal cry of adoration.

3. *Holy* expressed the mysterious, incalculable, unapproachable quality of the divine in contrast to the human. The threefold repetition suggests a superlative, 'Most holy' (cp. Jer. 7: 4). As applied to people and objects *holy* indicates their preparation for the divine service, primarily ritual separation. The enriched content of meaning that appears in 5: 16 is characteristic of Isaiah. *glory* is the word for the divine self-manifestation, associated with light, fire and storm as in Ezek. 1: 4–28. The thought in this verse appears in Pss. 57: 5, 11; 72: 19. It marked the divine appearance at the beginning of Israel's covenant relationship (Exod. 24: 16, 17). God elected Israel for his glory (Isa. 43: 7), and it is Israel's function to declare his glory among the nations (Ps. 96: 3). In fulfilment of the Old Testament hope there will be the universal acknowledgement of God's glory (Hab. 2: 14). If 'holiness' is the word for the unapproachable mystery of God, *glory* is the word for his manifestation in history and nature.

5. *I am lost:* since 'no mortal man may see me and live' (Exod. 33: 20), Isaiah is reduced to the silence and stillness of death. But this horror is not simply that of creature before the creator, but of a sinful man before holy perfection. The specific reference to the *lips,* is to that part of the body which most characterizes him who would join in the worship of God. Yet even in the highly individual experience, he is one with his *people.* If he is to be consecrated as prophet (8f.), it is not to be separated from them, but to be the living heart of his people. So the work of divine cleansing (6f.) is not for himself alone but the beginning of his people's cleansing.

8. *Who will go for me?* The Hebrew pronoun is 'for us'. Isaiah is taken into the heavenly council in which the divine decrees are made known (cp. 1 Kings 22: 19; Jer. 23: 18, 22). He is to be the messenger of the divine king.

9. *this people:* instead of *my* people, since by their conduct they have abandoned the right to be the people of God. They

have rebelled and must expect to be treated as hostile aliens. The private oracle to the newly commissioned prophet was all too tragically realized in his subsequent ministry. The warnings were disregarded, the messages rejected. Yet they must be given. The Hebrew of verse 10 is harsher than the N.E.B.: 'Dull their wits, make them deaf and blind lest they see, listen and understand.' What is emphasized is the terrible inevitability which rejection of God produces. Distrust, disobedience, disloyalty produces a moral and spiritual insensitiveness so that the presence of God is seen as threat and destruction. It may be noted that this passage is referred to in each of the Gospels (cp. Matt. 13: 14–15 etc.) and twice by Paul (Acts 28: 26–7; Rom. 11–8). Yet against this inevitable judgement the prophet can still utter the liturgical (Ps. 74: 10) 'How long?' The answer is the same: 'Until everything is lost' (verses 11–13a). History was to show that there was a further divine word beyond this, and appropriately this was added to the book of the eighth-century prophet in Isa. 40ff., for this too was the result at last of the prophet's word.

13b is in brackets. Both the text and its meaning are obscure. If it is original to Isaiah, it can only be read as a further description of utter destruction. It could be rendered: 'like an oak and a terebinth which when they are felled have in them a stump. A holy seed is its stump.' This, though obscure, sounds like a later comment adding a word of hope. This sentence is absent from the Septuagint, but the Greek modified 12b to mean 'and those who were left on the land were multiplied', a similarly hopeful note. ✳

Prophecies during the Syro-Ephraimite war

THE SIGN OF SHEAR-JASHUB

WHILE AHAZ SON OF JOTHAM and grandson of 7
Uzziah was king of Judah, Rezin king of Aram
with Pekah son of Remaliah, king of Israel, marched on
Jerusalem, but could not force a battle. When the house 2
of David heard that the Aramaeans had come to terms
with the Ephraimites, king and people were shaken like
forest trees in the wind. Then the LORD said to Isaiah, Go 3
out with your son Shear-jashub[a] to meet Ahaz at the end
of the conduit of the Upper Pool by the causeway leading
to the Fuller's Field, and say to him, Be on your guard, 4
keep calm; do not be frightened or unmanned by these
two smouldering stumps of firewood, because Rezin and
his Aramaeans with Remaliah's son are burning with rage.
The Aramaeans with Ephraim and Remaliah's son have 5
laid their plans against you, saying, Let us invade Judah 6
and break her spirit;[b] let us make her join with us, and
set the son of Tabeal on the throne. Therefore the Lord 7
GOD has said:

> This shall not happen now, and never shall,
> for all that the chief city of Aram is Damascus, 8
>   and Rezin is the chief of Damascus;
> within sixty-five years

[a] *That is* A remnant shall return.   [b] *Or* and parley with her.

Ephraim shall cease to be a nation,
9   for all that Samaria is the chief city of Ephraim,
and Remaliah's son the chief of Samaria.
Have firm faith, or you will not stand firm.

※ The events of the years 735–733 B.C. are described with greater detail in 2 Kings 16: 1–20. Jerusalem was besieged by the combined armies of Syria (Aram) and Israel. Apparently the intention was to force Judah into an alliance against Assyria; if Ahaz should prove unwilling, as he did, he would be replaced by a more compliant king, 'the son of Tabeal'. This name, as spelt, appears to be a deliberate distortion to mean 'good for nothing' for an original 'Tabel', meaning 'God is good'. He was a Syrian prince, but may have been a son of Uzziah by a Syrian princess. The attack was serious and was probably supported by Edomites and Philistines (2 Chron. 28: 16–18). The fears of the nation of Judah were understandable.

3. Isaiah was sent *to meet* the king as he was inspecting the water-supply for Jerusalem. He brought with him his *son Shear-jashub* – 'a remnant shall return'. The meaning is ambiguous, either a warning 'only a remnant' or a word of hope beyond disaster (as in 10: 20–1). The former is the meaning here, a warning of the consequences of the royal policy as described in 2 Kings 16: 7f.

4. Against this panic-stricken policy, the oracle is given. *Rezin* and Pekah may be hot with rage, but they are no more than two bits of wood still *smouldering* in a dying fire. This is followed by a further oracle with its triumphant conclusion in the last line, where the N.E.B. draws attention to the word-play in the Hebrew.

8. *within sixty-five years Ephraim shall cease to be a nation* is neither factually correct, nor relevant to the situation confronting Ahaz, and destroys the rhythm of the oracle. But it is difficult to understand what it meant when it was added. It

may have read originally 'within six or even five years' (so Jerusalem Bible). It is also possible that this part of verse 8 originally followed the first half of verse 9.

In fact Isaiah's words were disregarded. Ahaz relied upon the help of Assyria, and Tiglath-pileser did attack Israel and Syria. By 732 B.C. most of Israel and Syria was occupied by the Assyrians (2 Kings 16: 9; 15: 29). *

THE SIGN OF IMMANUEL

Once again the LORD spoke to Ahaz and said, Ask the 10, 11 LORD your God for a sign, from lowest Sheol or from highest heaven. But Ahaz said, No, I will not put the 12 LORD to the test by asking for a sign. Then the answer 13 came: Listen, house of David. Are you not content to wear out men's patience? Must you also wear out the patience of my God? Therefore the Lord himself shall 14 give you a sign: A young woman is with child, and she will bear a son, and will[a] call him Immanuel.[b] By the 15 time that he has learnt to reject evil and choose good, he will be eating curds and honey;[c] before that child has 16 learnt to reject evil and choose good, desolation will come upon the land before whose two kings you cower now. The LORD will bring on you, your people, and your 17 house, a time the like of which has not been seen since Ephraim broke away from Judah.[d]

* These verses are closely connected with the foregoing, and the incident probably took place a few days later. Since Ahaz apparently ignored Isaiah's warning, the prophet invited him

[a] *Or* you will.   [b] *That is* God is with us.
[c] he will...honey: *or* curds and honey will be eaten.
[d] *Prob. rdg.; Heb. adds* the king of Assyria.

to ask for any sign he liked to choose, however unlikely it might seem. Only one who had so completely given himself to be the Lord's messenger could dare to speak in such terms. Isaiah was himself the living exposition of faith. The reply of Ahaz sounds very pious, cp. Deut. 6: 16, but is in fact a rejection of the divine offer through the prophet. It is evident that Ahaz knew that the sign would be given, that it would point to a way of life already declared in verse 9, and therefore would condemn the policy, reliance upon Assyria, on which he was already determined.

The sign, however, will be given as unmistakable evidence of God's presence and activity in this situation. It will still point to the divine intention to deliverance from the attack of Rezin and Pekah (16), but, since it was rejected, it will continue into the disaster brought about by the Assyrian king upon whom Ahaz relied rather than upon God (17).

Behind the sign and its explication lie the promises to the Davidic dynasty preserved in 2 Sam. 7, 23: 1–7; Pss. 89, 110, 132, which formed part of the coronation ceremony. These promises required also a response of loyalty to God from the king. Ahaz was unable to believe in the promises because of his disloyalty. Therefore the sign of hope became the sign of disaster.

11. *a sign* may be any event, normal or abnormal, which may quicken the mind to perceive the divine action in a situation (cp. 1 Sam. 10: 2ff.; 1 Kings 13: 3–5).

14. *A young woman:* the Hebrew word, like the English, does not preclude the meaning of 'virgin' that appears in the Authorized Version, but usage would hardly suggest it. In any case, the young woman is not the sign; that is the son about to be born and given the significant name *Immanuel*, God is with us. Almost the same words occur in the Ras Shamra text (found at the ancient Ugarit on the Syrian coast) 'A young woman shall bear a son'; the noun is the same as in Hebrew. The point of the oracle is clear. A pregnant woman, probably one of Ahaz' wives, *will bear a son* with a name

which will give assurance of divine protection, yet, since this sign has been rejected, within a few years this same divine presence will bring the disastrous subservience to Assyria.

15. *curds and honey*. The exact significance is not clear. They may indicate desert conditions, and so privation; or they may suggest the food of the gods, or abundant food (Exod. 3: 8). But the length of time is indicated by the age at which the child would be able to *choose* what he likes and *reject* what he dislikes, i.e. within about three years.

16. *reject evil and choose good* is not used here to indicate moral responsibility, but the age of discrimination.

It may be noted that the warning of 17, disregarded by Ahaz, began to be realized with the Assyrian invasion of the northern kingdom in 733/2 B.C. and the consequent capitulation of Judah. Whatever hopes may have been cherished by the Davidic dynasty of regaining its sovereignty over all Israel, were annihilated. The words 'the king of Assyria' (verses 17, 20, N.E.B. footnote) were originally a marginal note of a later reader, correctly understanding the situation. ✷

ORACLES OF DEVASTATION

On that day the LORD will whistle for the fly from the distant streams of Egypt and for the bee from Assyria. 18

They shall all come and settle in the precipitous ravines 19
and in the clefts of the rock; camel-thorn and stinkwood shall be black with them. On that day the Lord shall shave 20
the head and body with a razor hired on the banks of the Euphrates,[a] and it shall remove the beard as well. On 21
that day a man shall save alive a young cow and two ewes; and he shall get so much milk that he eats curds; for all 22
who are left in the land shall eat curds and honey. On that 23
day every place where there used to be a thousand vines

[a] *Prob. rdg.; Heb. adds* with the king of Assyria.

worth a thousand pieces of silver shall be given over to
24 thorns and briars. A man shall go there only to hunt with
bow and arrows, for thorns and briars cover the whole
25 land; and no one who fears thorns and briars shall set
foot on any of those hills once worked with the hoe. Oxen
shall be turned loose on them, and sheep shall trample
them.

✳ There are four oracles, each introduced by 'on that day',
verses 18f., 20, 21f., 23–5, and they develop the warnings
indicated in the preceding section. 'That day' is not merely a
reference to time but an indication that what is to happen
is the appointed day of the Lord's judgement on his covenant
people.

18f. The land will become a battle-ground for the great
powers, Assyria and Egypt, a consequence of the inept state-
craft of the kings of Israel and Judah. Hosea (7: 11; 9: 3)
uttered the same warning. The specific reference to *the fly*
and *the bee* is appropriate. The flooding of the Nile brought
with it swarms of flies, and the hill districts of Assyria were
well known for their bees.

20. Ahaz supposed that he had *hired* Tiglath-pileser (2
Kings 16: 7f.); he would find that the Lord had *hired* him
for the downfall of Israel. The shaving of the hair, *the beard
as well*, was a mark of degradation (cp. 2 Sam. 10: 4f.).

21f. The land will be so devastated and depopulated that
it will go out of cultivation and provide only food for a few
rescued cattle. It will provide *curds and honey*, but no more.

23–5. A further threat of devastation. The cultivated land
reverts to jungle. So far as Judah was concerned, the threat
was not fulfilled in the reign of Ahaz, but was realized as a
consequence of Hezekiah's rebellion in 701 B.C. ✳

SPEED-SPOIL-HASTEN-PLUNDER

The LORD said to me, Take a large tablet and write on **8**
it in common writing,*a* Maher-shalal-hash-baz;*b* and **2**
fetch*c* Uriah the priest and Zechariah son of Jeberechiah
for me as trustworthy witnesses. Then I lay with the **3**
prophetess, and she conceived and bore a son; and the
LORD said to me, Call him Maher-shalal-hash-baz.
Before the boy can say Father or Mother, the wealth of **4**
Damascus and the spoils of Samaria shall be carried off
and presented to the king of Assyria.

* The warning and threats in 7: 1–25 were disregarded. Now
a further sign is given, of an even more explicit character.
To make it more emphatic, it is given two-fold expression.
The ominous name was first written down before two witnesses, and available for anyone to read. It was then given
living expression, as it was given to the prophet's son born
about a year later. The sign was not merely prediction as we
commonly understand that word. It was a divine act which,
through the response of the prophet, was initiating its own
fulfilment. The giving of the name to the new-born son,
himself the product of divine activity (cp. Ps. 139: 13–16),
reinforced the first sign. It is probably for this reason that
Isaiah's wife was called *the prophetess*; she too was the
bearer of the powerful word of the Lord. The prophetic sign
declared that within a year of the birth of the child, the kingdoms of *Damascus* and *Samaria* would be invaded by *Assyria*;
the prophecy was fulfilled in 733/2 B.C. *

[a] in common writing: *or* with an ordinary stylus.
[b] *That is* Speed-spoil–hasten-plunder.
[c] *So Scroll; Heb.* and I will fetch.

SHILOAH AND EUPHRATES

5 Once again the LORD said to me:

6   Because this nation has rejected
the waters of Shiloah, which run so softly and gently,[a]

7   therefore the Lord will bring up against it
    the strong, flooding waters of the Euphrates,
    the king of Assyria and all his glory;
    it shall run up all its channels
    and overthrow all its banks;

8   it shall sweep through Judah in a flood,
    pouring over it and rising shoulder-high.

✻ The point of this passage depends upon contrasts which would be immediately apparent to Isaiah's hearers, between the conduit from the Gihon spring (*the waters of Shiloah*) into Jerusalem, and the great river *Euphrates*. The former, springing mysteriously from the earth, was manifestly the Lord's gift to Jerusalem; it flowed continuously and quietly. The Gihon spring appears to have played some part in the coronation of the Davidic dynasty (1 Kings 1: 33f.), a further reminder of God's promises of protection. The Euphrates was a mighty river, often destructive in flood and wholly alien to Judah. So this nation, in rejecting the evidence of the Lord's care and protection, have chosen a power that is alien and destructive by calling to *Assyria* for help. Yet Isaiah saw even the apparently unruly Assyria to be under God's control. It is a vigorous and penetrating parable. (The reference in the footnote to the additional words at the end of verse 6 recognizes them as a later marginal note. It may have been misplaced from verse 12, where the word translated 'too hard' was understood as 'conspiracy', as it is translated at 2 Sam. 15: 12. The cognate verb is frequently translated 'to conspire'.) ✻

[a] *Prob. rdg.; Heb. adds* Rezin and the son of Remaliah.

IMMANUEL – GOD IS WITH US

The whole expanse of the land shall be filled,
so wide he spreads his wings; for God is with us.[a]
Take note,[b] you nations, and be dismayed.   9
Listen, all you distant parts of the earth:
you may arm yourselves but will be dismayed;
you may arm yourselves but will be dismayed.
Make your plans, but they will be foiled,   10
propose what you please, but it shall not stand;
for God is with us.[a]

* This appears to be part of a hymn of hope; cp. Ps. 46. The
outspread *wings* recall the words of Pss. 17: 8; 91: 4 as a
symbol of God's protection. Since *God is with us*, the attacks
of the enemy nations cannot succeed. This is Isaiah's confidence
which he vainly sought to communicate to Ahaz. If, as is
possible, Isaiah was quoting from a temple hymn, he was
recalling his people to their ancient faith. *

AN AUTOBIOGRAPHICAL NOTE

These were the words of the LORD to me, for his hand   11
was strong upon me; and he warned me not to follow[c]
the ways of this people: You shall not say 'too hard' of 12
everything that this people calls hard; you shall neither
dread nor fear that which they fear. It is the LORD of   13
Hosts whom you must count 'hard';[d] he it is whom you
must fear and dread. He shall become your 'hardship',[d] 14

[a] God is with us: *Heb.* Immanuel. [b] Take note: *so Sept.; Heb.
unintelligible.* [c] *Or* and he turned me from following... [d] 'hard'
and 'hardship': *prob. rdg.; Heb. unintelligible in this context.*

a boulder and a rock which the two houses of Israel shall
run against and over which they shall stumble, a trap and
15 a snare to those who live in Jerusalem; and many shall
stumble over them, many shall fall and be broken, many
shall be snared and caught.

16   Fasten up the message,
       seal the oracle with my teaching;[a]
17   and I will wait for the LORD
          who hides his face from the house of Jacob;
          I will watch for him.
18   See, I and the sons whom the LORD has given me
        are to be signs and portents in Israel,
     sent by the LORD of Hosts who dwells on Mount Zion.

✻ The persistent rejection of the word of the Lord through
his prophet can have only one consequence. Isaiah's public
ministry must cease. This is seen as a divine compulsion to
dissociate himself from God's people, for they have dissociated
themselves from God. The phrase 'for his hand was strong
upon me' may indicate a condition of ecstasy, as often in
Ezekiel, but in any case a deeply-felt compulsion. The prophet
must cease to be a prophet! Yet some have heeded his words,
and they must be confirmed in their faith-response. Forbidden
to engage in his public prophetic ministry, Isaiah became a
teacher of the faithful and entrusted them with a record of his
prophetic ministry until events should have fulfilled his words
and symbolic acts.

The passage is difficult both as to translation and as to
interpretation, as various versions indicate.

11. A divine word to the prophet himself.

12-15. These verses contain Isaiah's teaching to a small

[a] *Or* among my disciples, *or, with Sept.*, where it cannot be studied.

70

circle of those who believed; the verbs are second person plural. The word *hard*, twice in verse 12, usually means 'conspiracy'; *hard* and *hardship* in verses 13f. represent an emendation of the Hebrew which means 'treat as holy' and 'sanctuary' respectively (in written Hebrew the words are similar).

16. The N.E.B. rendering suggests another word of the Lord to Isaiah, and 17–18 his response. But verse 16 could be translated 'I will fasten up *the message*, seal *the oracle*' and *with my teaching* could be rendered 'among my disciples'; then the verses 16–18 as a whole could be Isaiah's response to the divine command in verse 11.

In spite of the difficulties in detail, the essential meaning is clear. Those who reject the word of the Lord are opposing the only ruler of history; they can only find God as hostile and the cause of their downfall. The prophet can only wait confidently for the fulfilment of the divine purpose and prepare a faithful remnant for that fulfilment. Much in the same way Jesus also, rejected by the many, prepared his disciples to receive the Kingdom. ✲

FRAGMENTS OF PROPHETIC ORACLES

But men will say to you,   19
'Seek guidance of ghosts and familiar spirits
    who squeak and gibber;
a nation may surely seek guidance of its gods,
of the dead on behalf of the living,
    for an oracle or a message?'   20
They will surely say some such thing as this;
    but what they say is futile.
So despondency and fear will come over them,   21
    and then, when they are afraid and fearful,
    they will turn against their king and their gods.

22   Then, whether they turn their gaze upwards or look
down,
everywhere is distress and darkness inescapable,
constraint and gloom that cannot be avoided;

9 1[a]   for there is no escape for an oppressed people.

For, while the first invader has dealt lightly with the
land of Zebulun and the land of Naphtali, the second has
dealt heavily with Galilee of the Nations on the road
beyond Jordan to the sea.

✶ The obscurity of this passage appears to be due to the fact
that we have three oracles incompletely preserved, yet
retained by Isaiah's disciples because they contained valued
words of the Lord. Because of their fragmentary condition,
interpretation must be tentative. It should be recognized that
the N.E.B. has rendered into intelligible English a passage
which in Hebrew is obscure; compare the Authorized Version,
the Revised Version, the Revised Standard Version and the
Jerusalem Bible for other renderings.

The passage might be divided as follows: 19–20, against
necromancy; 21–2, despair; 9: 1, invasion.

19–20. One of the striking features of Israel's faith even at
an early period, is its refusal to allow the consulting of the
spirits *of the dead*. It was intolerable to those who believed
in 'the living God'. It is when that faith is abandoned that
the cult of necromancy, or its modern equivalent in spiritual-
ism, flourishes. A people that seeks such 'gods' is as dead as
they are! We might put a full-stop at the end of verse 19
and render verse 20 'To the Torah and the Testimony!' i.e.
a recall to the true teaching of God; 'unless they say some
such thing as this there is no dawn for them'.

21–2. Appears to be part of an oracle describing the despair

[a] *8: 23 in Heb.*

of the people when the irresistible might of the Assyrian army overwhelmed the northern kingdom. The first impulse is to blame the king who cannot help, and God who will not.

9:1. A historical note describing two stages in Tiglath-pileser's invasion, referred to here in order to introduce the great oracle of hope that follows. In 733/2, the northern part of Israel (Galilee) was taken, and became an Assyrian province. *of the Nations*: this phrase indicates that the population of Galilee had a considerable non-Israelite element.   ✴

LIGHT SHINES IN THE DARKNESS

The people who walked in darkness   2[a]
have seen a great light:
light has dawned upon them,
    dwellers in a land as dark as death.
Thou hast increased their joy and[b] given them great   3
    gladness;
they rejoice in thy presence as men rejoice at harvest,
or as they are glad when they share out the spoil;
    for thou hast shattered the yoke that burdened them, 4
    the collar that lay heavy on their shoulders,
    the driver's goad, as on the day of Midian's defeat.
    All the boots of trampling soldiers   5
    and the garments fouled with blood
shall become a burning mass, fuel for fire.
For a boy has been born for us, a son given to us   6
    to bear the symbol of dominion on his shoulder;
      and he shall be called
      in purpose wonderful, in battle God-like,
      Father for all time,[c] Prince of peace.

[a] *9: 1 in Heb.*   [b] *their joy and: prob. rdg.; Heb.* the nation, not.
[c] *Or* of a wide realm.

7   Great^a shall the dominion be,
        and boundless the peace
    bestowed on David's throne and on his kingdom,
    to establish it and sustain it
        with justice and righteousness
        from now and for evermore.
    The zeal of the LORD of Hosts shall do this.

✷ There is a high degree of artistic skill and theological insight in placing this hymn to follow the preceding section. Man has sunk to the depths; political events have made his condition hopeless. But God's creative word is about to bring light into the chaos that man has produced. In the narrower sense it is not a prophetic oracle, but a hymn of praise to God expressing faith in the fulfilment of the divine purpose. It resembles indeed those psalms that celebrate the accession of a king of the Davidic dynasty, e.g. Pss. 21; 89: 1–37. In the high moment of worship, the people of God become a prophetic community. Such a hymn could have partial fulfilments, or stages of fulfilment in the history of this people; Hezekiah and Josiah are obvious examples. It became an essential element in Jewish messianic expectation, especially during the centuries after the exile when no king ruled in Jerusalem. Christians have rightly seen the fulfilment of the hymn in the life and work of Jesus (cp. Matt. 4: 14–16) and the Church has associated this passage together with Isa. 11: 1–10 with the celebration of the Nativity. The hymn, then, may be seen as relating to a particular situation, or to more than one. But it also prepares the mind and strengthens the confidence in the fulfilment of God's purpose towards which he is working in history. What is expressed here is not 'wishful thinking' but a certainty based on God's active rule in the affairs of mankind. The hymn may well have been composed by Isaiah, the prophet whose vision is recorded in ch. 6, who received

[a] *So Sept.; Heb. prefixes two unintelligible letters.*

74

the Immanuel oracle. Certainly it would be appropriate to the darkness and gloom of Assyrian invasion. Clearly the 'new-born king' is not Ahaz, but it might well express hopes centred on Hezekiah who may have been co-regent with Ahaz for some years before the latter's death.

2. *darkness:* the language of this verse is used in Job 10: 21f.; 38: 17 of the underworld inhabited by the dead; i.e. the people are threatened with extinction. This is what makes the contrast in verse 3 so vivid. God is about to restore them to life (cp. Ps. 4: 7).

4. A reference to the incident recorded in Judg. 7. A similar passage to these verses appears in Isa. 17: 12–14.

6. *has been born* may be literally understood, but more probably refers to the accession day of the king who on that day becomes by adoption God's son (Ps. 2: 7; cp. 2 Sam. 7: 14). The giving of the great names in this verse resembles Egyptian practice at the accession of the new Pharoah. Just as Isaiah was commanded to give names to his sons which were understood to bring about in history what the names meant, so the names of the king who is to come are given. He will be for the people of God what these names signify. The names have an inherent power of fulfilment. The first name is *in purpose wonderful* or Wonderful Counsellor. Normally a counsellor would be an official who advised the king, cp. 1: 26. This royal name suggests that the king will display incomparable and successful statesmanship. The second name, *in battle God-like* or Divine Warrior, declares that he will be victorious in battle against the enemies of his people. *Father for all time* describes the nature of his rule; he would be a true vice-gerent of God, fulfilling the coronation prayer of Ps. 72, and not a despot. A possible, though less likely, translation of this name is: Possessor of booty. This would mean that being successful in war, he would capture the wealth of his enemies. The last name, *Prince of peace*, means that he would give his kingdom that security in which peace and prosperity would be assured. The expectations contained in

75

these names were never realized in ancient Israel, but became a powerful element in Jewish messianic hopes.

7. This recalls the words of Ps. 21: 1–7. ✳

Prophecies addressed to Israel

THE OUTSTRETCHED ARM OF THE LORD

8 The Lord has sent forth his word against Jacob
    and it shall fall on Israel;
9   all the people shall be humbled,
    Ephraim and the dwellers in Samaria,
    though in their pride and arrogance they say,
10 The bricks are fallen, but we will build in hewn stone;
    the sycomores are hacked down,
    but we will use cedars instead.
11 The LORD has raised their foes[a] high against them
    and spurred on their enemies,
12 Aramaeans from the east and Philistines from the west,
    and they have swallowed Israel in one mouthful.
    For all this his anger has not turned back,
    and his hand is stretched out still.
13   Yet the people did not come back to him who struck them,
    or seek guidance of the LORD of Hosts;
14 therefore on one day the LORD cut off from Israel
head and tail, palm and reed.[b]
16 This people's guides have led them astray;

[a] their foes: *prob. rdg.; Heb.* the foes of Rezin. [b] *Prob. rdg.; Heb. adds* (15) The aged and honoured are the head, and the prophet who gives false instruction is the tail.

those who should have been guided are in confusion.

Therefore the Lord showed no mercy to their young 17
men,
no tenderness to their orphans and widows;
all were godless and evildoers,
every one speaking profanity.
For all this his anger has not turned back,
and his hand is stretched out still.

Wicked men have been set ablaze like a fire 18
fed with briars and thorns,
kindled in the forest thickets;
they are wrapped in a murky pall of smoke.
The land is scorched by the fury of the LORD of Hosts, 19
and the people have become fuel for the fire.*
On the right, one man eats his fill but yet is hungry; 20
on the left, another devours but is not satisfied;
each feeds on his own children's flesh,
and neither spares his own brother.*
*For all this his anger has not turned back, 21
and his hand is stretched out still.

Shame on you! you who make unjust laws **10**
and publish burdensome decrees,
depriving the poor of justice, 2
robbing the weakest of my people of their rights,
despoiling the widow and plundering the orphan.
What will you do when called to account, 3

[a] *See note on verse 20.*
[b] and neither...brother: *transposed from end of verse 19.*
[c] *Prob. rdg.; Heb. prefixes* Manasseh devours Ephraim, and Ephraim
Manasseh; together they are against Judah.

when ruin from afar confronts you?
To whom will you flee for help
and where will you leave your children,
4 so that they do not cower before the gaoler
  or fall by the executioner's hand?
For all this his anger has not turned back,
and his hand is stretched out still.

[24^a] So, as tongues of fire lick up the stubble
  and the heat of the flame dies down,
  their root shall moulder away,
  and their shoots vanish like dust;
 for they have spurned the instruction of the LORD of
  Hosts
 and have rejected the word of the Holy One of Israel.
[25^a] So the anger of the LORD is roused against his people,
 he has stretched out his hand against them and struck
  them down;
  the mountains trembled,
 and their corpses lay like offal in the streets.
 For all this his anger has not turned back,
 and his hand is stretched out still.

✻ This section is concerned with the northern kingdom. It is closely related to 5: 8–30. In particular the refrain at the end of each prophecy of doom, 9: 8–12, 13–17, 18–21, 10: 1–4 is repeated at the end of 5: 24–5; hence the inclusion of these last verses to follow 10: 1–4 in the N.E.B. It is also possible that the whole of 5: 24–30 should be associated with this section. Much in Hosea 4–13 is parallel to these oracles of doom. Since the divine judgement is uttered but not yet completed in this section, the prophecies must come before

[a] *These are verses 24 and 25 of ch. 5, transposed to this point.*

the final downfall of the northern kingdom in 721 but may reflect the devastation caused by the Assyrian invasion and the political chaos that followed after 734 B.C. Divine judgement is passed on account of pride, rejection of the Lord of the covenant, and gross social injustice.

8–12. The aftermath of invasion. The devastation caused by the invading army was met by hysterical boasting based, as it had been in the days of Amos, on a quite unrealistic confidence in divine protection, unrealistic because Israel had in fact forsaken God. Nothing is otherwise known of the events described in verse 12a, but it would be natural enough for Israel's neighbours to take advantage of her weakened condition. Isaiah's point, however, is that these events are not rightly to be understood solely in political terms. They have come because the powerful and active word of God has been sent into the historical situation to bring about those events. This is what lies at the heart of prophetic prediction. The divine word is filled with the power to effect its fulfilment. The prophet did not think of fate, but of an active God at work in human affairs to effect his righteous purpose. To neglect or reject this was to invite disaster.

13–17. Blind guides. Disaster might have awakened Israel to a genuine penitence and a return to their ancient faith. Instead, having rejected the words of their true prophets, they could only plunge into worse confusion and disaster. The 'young men' were the soldiers killed in battle, leaving behind them the widows and orphans. It is a familiar picture of unworthy leaders bringing misery upon the whole society. The word for 'godless' is a positive word meaning that they have polluted the God–man relationship, and this can only bring about the hostility of the Holy God.

14. *head and tail, palm and reed* is a vivid way of saying 'everybody, government and people'.

15. This verse appears in the footnotes as a scribal explanation which, however true in fact, is hardly appropriate to 'head and tail'.

18–21. Political and social chaos. This section describes the rapid progress of unchecked evil and violence. The result is the inevitable breakdown of society. But again this is to be explained not simply in sociological terms, but as a direct consequence of hostility to God against evil and those who choose evil. Politically this manifested itself in the civil wars referred to in 2 Kings 15: 8–16: 30. It is apparently to these that the note at the beginning of 21 refers (see footnote *c*). It is not certain whether these words are from Isaiah, or a later commentator, but they are appropriate to the historical situation.

1–4. Unjust law-makers. This section suggests the grief of the prophet as he surveyed the scene he has described. The tone of these verses is, while no less condemnatory, sorrowful. While the closing words associate this section with 9: 8–21, the opening exclamation (one word in Hebrew, corresponding to the grief-stricken word of Jesus in Luke 11: 42–52) picks up the same words in 5: 8–23. The doom is inevitable for those who have ruled with injustice, blatantly using their power to oppress those who cannot defend themselves. But the prophet is a man of his people, pronouncing the doom with a grief and sorrow that reflects the divine sorrow.

2. *despoiling the widow and plundering the orphan:* the widow and the orphan in ancient societies were particularly vulnerable, lacking a man to guard their rights in the law-court.

3. *ruin from afar* refers to the Assyrian army, but it may have a hidden reference to the God whom they by their conduct have made *afar*. For they were wantonly breaking their divinely inspired law (Exod. 22: 22–4); was not their God known as 'father of the fatherless and the widow's champion' (Ps. 68: 5)?

24–5. The final catastrophe. The first word, *So* (Hebrew 'therefore'), suggests that the opening words describing the charge have been lost; we have only the Judge's sentence. It does not logically follow from 10: 4, or from 5: 23, but it could be said to follow 9: 20 and to pick up the words of

9: 18, 19. It is probably best to regard these verses as a fragmentary oracle, and as a conclusion to the series. The verses
undoubtedly describe the end of a people who have *spurned
the instruction* or rejected God's *torah* (? Exod. 20–3). *

WOE TO THE SELF-SUFFICIENT ASSYRIAN

The Assyrian! He is the rod that I wield in my anger, 5
and the staff of my wrath is in his hand.[a]
I send him against a godless nation, 6
I bid him march against a people who rouse my
    wrath,
to spoil and plunder at will
and trample them down like mud in the streets.
But this man's purpose is lawless, 7
lawless are the plans in his mind;
   for his thought is only to destroy
and to wipe out nation after nation.
'Are not my officers all kings?' he says; 8
   'see how Calno has suffered the fate of Carchemish. 9
Is not Hamath like Arpad, and Samaria like Damascus?
Before now I have found kingdoms full of idols, 10
   with more images than Jerusalem and Samaria,
and now, what I have done to Samaria and her worth- 11
   less gods,
I will do also to Jerusalem and her idols.'

When the Lord has finished all that he means to do on 12
Mount Zion and in Jerusalem, he[b] will punish the king of
Assyria for this fruit of his pride and for his arrogance
and vainglory, because he said: 13

[a] and...hand: *prob. rdg.; Heb. obscure.*
[b] *So Sept.; Heb.* I.

By my own might I have acted
and in my own wisdom I have laid my schemes;
I have removed the frontiers of nations
   and plundered their treasures,
like a bull I have trampled on their inhabitants.

14   My hand has found its way to the wealth of nations,
and, as a man takes the eggs from a deserted nest,
so have I taken every land;
not a wing fluttered,
not a beak gaped, no chirp was heard.

15   Shall the axe set itself up against the hewer,
or the saw claim mastery over the sawyer,
as if a stick were to brandish him who wields it,
or a staff of wood to wield one who is not wood?

✳ In this passage, Isaiah's understanding of the meaning of history and of the active rule of God in all human affairs is clearly demonstrated. It is, of course, declared in quite concrete and specific terms, not in general propositions. This is characteristic of prophetic teaching. He does not provide a general formula which we can apply to any situation. Rather does he present us with a series of pictures which can quicken the understanding and moral insight of those who have eyes to see and thus enable his hearers to assess rightly their own situation whether in the eighth century B.C. or the twentieth century A.D. For the prophet would insist that the same God with the same holy purpose is at work throughout. The prophet's words must first be read against his world situation and the world outlook of his day.

The passage is not dated. It must be after the fall of Samaria in 722 (verse 11) and when Jerusalem was threatened. This would point to the time of Hezekiah's revolt against Sennacherib, 705-701, although an earlier date is possible, such as the time of Hezekiah's first revolt 713–711 against Sargon II. In either case the situation is clear. The Judaean state was threatened with invasion by the army of the great power, Assyria, before which it was, humanly speaking, helpless. But this was not merely a politically hopeless situation; it was a denial of all that the religion of this people held dear. For if Assyria was victorious, as was virtually certain, this could only mean that God was unable to protect his people or to exercise effective rule in his land. True, there were those who buoyed themselves up with hope by recalling the words of their temple prayers like Ps. 27; apparently Hezekiah was one of those at the beginning of the revolt. But like so much popular religion everywhere, it was quite unrealistic. It was based on the simple argument: we are his people, therefore he is bound to protect us; if he does not, he is obviously impotent.

The prophetic faith in this situation was utterly opposed to popular religion; indeed it must have sounded like madness to his contemporaries. Perhaps only the continuing history of this people could make it evident that he was inspired, for what he had to say can hardly be accounted for in terms of human judgement or reason.

Assyria, like other great powers in history, was aggressive, brutal and ruthless in pursuit of its imperial goals. It believed it had a great destiny to which the national deity Ashur was directing it, that of world conquest. Its king was the Great King. Small nations and their deities must acknowledge his sovereignty. Isaiah reversed all this. First it was Yahweh, God of Israel, who was directing the Assyrian king, and it was for the special purpose of chastising his own impenitent people. This was a logical consequence of Isaiah's inaugural vision of Yahweh the exalted king whose glory filled the earth. In this situation he recalled the name he had given to his second son, Spoil and Plunder (10: 6; cp. 8: 2), earlier a word of encouragement to the Judaeans, but now a threat. There is one, and only one sovereign and directing power in human affairs; and that is God whose power was never seen more clearly than in his own people's defeat. Secondly, because Assyria is a tool but also a sentient tool arrogantly claiming the right to do what he likes, God will humble him. It is a striking fact that the Greek poets as well as Israel's prophets saw arrogance and tyranny as utterly destructive, though the Greeks saw this in relation to fate while the prophets saw this in relation to God's holy purpose for man. The Assyrians themselves saw something of this, at any rate in other peoples, as it appears from the records of Sennacherib's successor. What is remarkable is that Isaiah dares to make this affirmation about Yahweh who was to all appearances a defeated and discredited deity. With this passage, compare also Isa. 14: 24–7; 31: 8f.; 37: 22–9.

5. The verse actually begins with a cry of lamentation, indicating sorrow for the fate of Assyria of which its proud king was unaware.

9. *Calno* had been conquered in 738, *Carchemish* in 717, *Arpad* in 738, *Hamath* in 720, *Samaria* in 722, *Damascus* in 732.

10–11. From the point of view of the Assyrian king, Yahweh of Israel is not essentially different from other national deities.

12. This is in prose and may be due to a later commentator, but possibly based on an Isaiah oracle at the end of the verse. In the Hebrew text, the pronoun is 'I' (see footnote).

13. We should understand by *might* and *wisdom* his military resources and the advice of his wise men who had consulted the stars for favourable omens. *removed the frontiers* indicates Assyrian imperial policy, which was to destroy national differences by uniting various small states into one province. But it was also a violation of what was understood throughout the world, including Assyria, as divinely appointed order (cp. Deut. 32: 8).

15 is a wisdom saying in parabolic form. It invites the response 'Of course not' and so exposes the hearer to self-judgement (cp. Matt. 7: 16). Similar passages are used by other prophets, e.g. Amos 3: 3–6, and are known in extra-biblical literature. ✶

AGAINST ASSYRIA

Therefore the Lord, the LORD of Hosts, will send disease 16
    on his sturdy frame, from head to toe,*[a]*
and within his flesh*[b]* a fever like fire shall burn.
    The light of Israel shall become a fire 17
        and his Holy One a flame,
which in one day shall burn up and consume
        his thorns and his briars;
the glory of forest and meadow shall be destroyed 18
        as when a man falls in a fit;
    and the remnant of trees in the forest shall be so few 19
        that a child may count them one by one.

On that day the remnant of Israel, the survivors of 20
Jacob, shall cease to lean on him that proved their destroyer,
but shall loyally lean on the LORD, the Holy One of Israel.

    A remnant shall turn again, a remnant of Jacob, 21
        to God their champion.
Your people, Israel, may be many as the sands of the sea, 22
        but only a remnant shall turn again,
    the instrument of final destruction,
        justice in full flood;*[c]*
for the Lord, the LORD of Hosts, will bring final 23
        destruction
    upon all the earth.

Therefore these are the words of the Lord, the LORD 24
of Hosts: My people who live in Zion, you must not be
afraid of the Assyrians, though they beat you with their

[a] from...toe; *transposed from verse 18; lit.* from neck to groin.
[b] within his flesh: *or* in his strong body.   [c] the instrument...flood:
or wasting with sickness, yet overflowing with righteousness.

rod and lift their staff against you as the Egyptians did;
25 for soon, very soon, my anger will come to an end, and
26 my wrath will all be spent.[a] Then the LORD of Hosts will
brandish his whip over them as he did when he struck
Midian at the Rock of Oreb, and will lift his staff against
the River as he did against Egypt.

27   On that day
        the burden they laid on your shoulder shall be
           removed
        and their yoke shall be broken from your neck.
28 An invader from Rimmon[b] has come to Aiath,
        has passed by Migron,
        and left his baggage-train at Michmash;
29   he has passed by Maabarah
        and camped for the night at Geba.
Ramah is anxious, Gibeah of Saul is in panic.
30   Raise a shrill cry, Bath-gallim;
hear it, Laish, and answer her, Anathoth:
31 'Madmenah is in flight; take refuge, people of Gebim.'
32 Today he is due to pitch his camp in Nob;
        he gives the signal to advance
        against the mount of the daughter of Zion,
        the hill of Jerusalem.

33   Look, the Lord, the LORD of Hosts,
        cleaves the trees with a flash of lightning,
the tallest are hewn down, the lofty laid low,
34   the heart of the forest is felled with the axe,
        and Lebanon with its noble trees has fallen.

[a] will...spent: *prob. rdg.; Heb. obscure.* [b] and their yoke...Rim-
mon: *prob. rdg.; Heb.* and their yoke from upon your neck, and a yoke
shall be broken because of oil. He...

✱ The connection between these verses and those that precede and follow is not obvious, and they appear to be a collection of independent oracles. As the N.E.B. footnotes show, translation is sometimes difficult and the text uncertain. Note that the opening clause of verse 28 is not only an emendation but in the Hebrew text is the conclusion of verse 27 (cp. English versions). The passage may be divided as follows: 16–19, the fire of God; 20, a prophecy of hope in prose; 21–3, the repentant remnant; 24–7, fear not Assyria; 28–32, the march of the invader; 33–4, the divine Forester.

16–19. The fire of God. The present position of these verses describes the fate that will fall upon the proud Assyrian, but the language is more appropriate as a judgement on the northern kingdom of Israel (cp. 9: 18; 5: 24; Ps. 83: 14) where forest fires were a serious danger during the dry summer. Thus as a raging *fever* wastes the body, so will the fiery *flame* devastate the forest land and pastures. But a terrible paradox is here. For it is the light of Israel, her guide (2: 4; Ps. 27: 1) and the Holy One, her only source of strength (12: 6), who has become the destroyer.

20. This is probably a recollection in prose rather than an exact record of the prophetic oracle. The disaster, either that of 722 when the northern kingdom was destroyed, or that of 701 (or possibly 586) when the Judaean kingdom had been invaded by Sennacherib (or Nebuchadnezzar), had taken place. Yet in the midst of disaster, there was hope for the loyal. *the remnant* is a link-word between verses 19 and 21, and indicates the way in which a prophet's oracles were remembered and transmitted by the disciples.

21–3. The repentant *remnant*. The prophetic name, Shearjashub (7: 3), is again recalled with *A remnant shall turn again*, but with a new significance. The survivors will be few, yet the means of divine judgement on the whole of mankind. This is most probably an oracle of a post-exilic prophet from the Isaianic circle. It points to God's final and decisive work in which those who trust in God the *champion* will return from exile.

87

24-7. Fear not Assyria. This oracle appears to relate to the Assyrian invasion under Sennacherib and so to date from the final period of Isaiah's ministry. Evidently (verse 24) the invasion has taken place, but while the prophet insists that this is in consequence of God's wrath, he is confident that release will come. To that end he reminds the people of their ancient tradition of God's saving work at the exodus and at the time of their settlement in Canaan. The language of verse 27 so closely resembles that of 14: 25 that the emendation may be confidently accepted.

28-32. The march of the *invader*. These verses vividly describe the march of an invading army, advancing through Benjamite territory towards Jerusalem. The context would suggest the Assyrian army, but the route taken by the Assyrians would normally be by the coastal plain. Since there are also some points of resemblance to Hos. 5: 8-12, it appears that this originally described the attack of Pekah and Rezin in the days of Ahaz, and should be associated with 7: 1-9. The sharp staccato phrases indicate urgency and are intended as a call to return to God before it is too late.

33-4. The divine Forester. There can be no certainty about the original setting of this oracle. It could refer to Israel in 734 or Judah in 701. The present context makes it an effective introduction to 11: 1-9. *

GOD'S ANOINTED AND THE RULE OF PEACE

11   Then a shoot shall grow from the stock of Jesse,
                and a branch shall spring[a] from his roots.

2   The spirit of the LORD shall rest upon him,
                a spirit of wisdom and understanding,
                a spirit of counsel[b] and power,
                a spirit of knowledge and the fear of the LORD.[c]

[a] *So Sept.; Heb.* bear fruit.   [b] *Or* force.
[c] *Prob. rdg.; Heb. adds* and his delight shall be in the fear of the LORD.

He shall not judge by what he sees   3
nor decide by what he hears;
he shall judge the poor with justice   4
and defend the humble in the land with equity;
his mouth shall be a rod to strike down the ruthless,[a]
and with a word he shall slay the wicked.
Round his waist he shall wear the belt of justice,   5
and good faith shall be the girdle round his body.
Then the wolf shall live with the sheep,   6
and the leopard lie down with the kid;
the calf and the young lion shall grow up[b] together,
and a little child shall lead them;
the cow and the bear shall be friends,   7
and their young shall lie down together.
The lion shall eat straw like cattle;
the infant shall play over the hole of the cobra,   8
and the young child dance over the viper's nest.
They shall not hurt or destroy in all my holy mountain; 9
for as the waters fill the sea,
so shall the land be filled with the knowledge of the
    LORD.

* Clearly this should be read in connection with 9: 2–7.
The word 'anointed' (Messiah) does not actually appear in
these verses, but it is implied in the description of the investiture of the Davidic king (cp. Ps. 72: 1–7). The qualities
described are those which were hoped for, and so rarely
realized, at each coronation. Yet this hope was strangely
persistent, and the New Testament sees it fulfilled in Jesus.
Whether the poem was composed by Isaiah, quoted or adapted
by him from a temple psalm, or included here by the disciple

[a] *Prob. rdg.; Heb.* land.
[b] shall grow up: *so Sept.; Heb.* and the buffalo.

who edited this collection of prophecies, it is impossible to say. In the light of the coronation psalms (especially Pss. 132, 145), an eighth-century date is quite possible, but it is one of those passages that acquired new depths of meaning in the post-exilic age when the Jews waited for the consolation of Israel. The quotation of parts of verses 6, 7, and 9 in Isa. 65: 25 applies these words to the restored Jewish community after the exile, while Hab. 2: 14 quotes verse 9 as a word of hope in the dark days of Babylonian oppression.

1. It is probably reading too much into the opening sentence to suppose it to mean that the Davidic dynasty has come to an end. Every Judaean king was a David, just as every Roman emperor was a Caesar (originally a personal name). But it does refer to a new king, and in Isaiah's day this could well have meant Hezekiah.

2. *The spirit*, i.e. the divine energy, will remain with the king permanently (cp. 1 Sam. 16: 13) to enable him rightly to direct the life of his people, to protect them when they are attacked and maintain him (and therefore his people) in a right relationship with God (knowledge and reverence).

3–5. The opening clause is omitted in the N.E.B. (see footnote *c*); it was probably an alternative reading in the Hebrew. The effective administration of justice was an essential characteristic of true kingship (cp. 2 Sam. 23: 3f.; Ps. 72: 1f.; Isa. 32: 1–8); this included compassion for the weak and punishment of the oppressor.

6–9. A description of the restoration of the divine purpose in creation which will come about when right and responsible government is established. This association between what we should call the natural order and human response to God is a frequent theme in the Old Testament, especially in the prophets (cp. Hos. 2: 18–23) and psalms, and is echoed by Paul in Rom. 8: 22. It should be added that in Palestine this was a quite practical thought, since flocks and herds were always liable to attack from wild beasts; a shepherd needed to be courageous (cp. 1 Sam. 17: 34–6). The climax of this passage

is in the last line of verse 9 where *knowledge of the LORD*
means that intimate relationship with God born of genuine
trust and obedience. ✻

A GLORIOUS FUTURE

On that day a scion from the root of Jesse   10
shall be set up as a signal to the peoples;
the nations shall rally to it,
and its resting-place shall be glorious.

On that day the Lord will make his power more glorious 11
by recovering the remnant of his people, those who are
still left, from Assyria and Egypt, from Pathros, from Cush
and Elam, from Shinar, Hamath and the islands of the sea.

Then he will raise a signal to the nations   12
   and gather together those driven out of Israel;
   he will assemble Judah's scattered people
   from the four corners of the earth.
   Ephraim's jealousy shall vanish,   13
   and Judah's enmity shall be done away.
   Ephraim shall not be jealous of Judah,
   nor Judah the enemy of Ephraim.
They shall swoop down on the Philistine flank in the west 14
   and together they shall plunder the tribes of the east;
   Edom and Moab shall be within their grasp,
   and Ammon shall obey them.
The LORD will divide the tongue of the Egyptian sea   15
   and wave his hand over the River
     to bring a scorching wind;
   he shall split it into seven channels
   and let men go across dry-shod.

16   So there shall be a causeway for the remnant of his
            people,
        for the remnant rescued from Assyria,
      as there was for Israel when they came up out of Egypt.

✻ 10. A later oracle, probably post-exilic, in which the Davidic
king in the day of judgement will be a rallying point for all the
nations who shall come to seek a word of the Lord. The Hebrew
includes a word which commonly means 'to seek an oracle'.

11. The return. This verse presupposes the dispersion of
God's people throughout Mesopotamia and Egypt and can
be read as a prose introduction to the following oracle. The
rendering of the N.E.B. is somewhat free and includes a
necessary emendation. By *more glorious* is meant an even
greater exodus. It might be possible to regard the words *from
Pathros...sea* as a later addition extending the original oracle
in the light of the sixth-century exile. Pathros is Upper Egypt;
Cush is Ethiopia; Elam is east of Babylonia; Shinar is Babylonia; Hamath is part of Syria. *islands of the sea* are the
Mediterranean islands, or possibly the Phoenician coastlands.

12–16. The new exodus. Again a post-exilic oracle of salvation and hope. The catch-word *signal* links this with verse 10.
It speaks of a new exodus, a united Israel and a new 'invasion'
of Canaan until the old Davidic kingdom is re-established.
Not only the Red Sea, but also the mighty Euphrates will be
dried up to enable the exiles to pass over in safety. There are
points of resemblance to Isa. 49: 22. ✻

TWO PSALMS

12   You shall say on that day:
            I will praise thee, O LORD,
            though thou hast been angry with me;
            thy anger has turned back,[a]

            [a] *So Sept.; Heb.* let thy anger turn back.

> and thou hast comforted me.
>> God is indeed my deliverer.   2
>> I am confident and unafraid;
> for the LORD is my refuge and defence[a]
>> and has shown himself my deliverer.
> And so you shall draw water with joy   3
>> from the springs of deliverance.

> You shall all say on that day: 4
> Give thanks to the LORD and invoke him by name,
>> make his deeds known in the world around;
>> declare that his name is supreme.
> Sing psalms to the LORD, for he has triumphed, 5
>> and this must be made known in all the world.
> Cry out, shout aloud, you that dwell in Zion,   6
> for the Holy One of Israel is among you in majesty.

✻ These two psalms, 1f. and 3–6, fittingly conclude the first main section of Isaiah's oracles uttered at a time of national disaster. Beyond, and even within, the tragedy there is hope for the future. God is now, as he was in the beginning the deliverer, and in the worshipful recognition of him as Saviour lies the certainty that all the world will acknowledge him. In the N.E.B. verse 3 is attached to 1–2, but the verb is plural, as in 4–6.

The first psalm begins with a call to worship in the second person singular. *on that day* is primarily the day of God's victory over all opposition to his purpose, and in this context the day of the new exodus. Originally verses 1–2 were part of an individual thanksgiving, now sung by all the new Israel. The second is a communal hymn (plural verbs) introduced by a rubric referring to some ritual act performed at the New

[a] defence: *prob. rdg.*, *cp. Sept.*; *Heb.* defence of Yah.

Year Festival at the Gihon spring (cp. Ps. 36: 8), by which acted symbol Israel expressed its confidence in the coming of the rain upon which all life depends. But this life-giving water is God's gift to mankind, which Israel knows, and in adoration must declare. ✷

Prophecies relating to foreign nations

✷ This section consists of 13: 1 – 23: 18. Most of the prophets of whose words we have an extended record, spoke words of judgement against foreign nations. To begin with, such oracles were related to the nations whose borders touched those of Israel (cp. Amos 1: 3 – 2: 3). But as this people were inevitably involved in the policies of the great powers, Egypt and Mesopotamia, so the prophetic vision widened to include them within the scope of God's sovereignty. This, with reference to Assyria, we have already seen in the preceding section of the book of Isaiah. This section is, in the main, composed of oracles relating to foreign nations. 'Oracle' is in fact a distinctive title attached to the various prophecies, occurring ten times in this section and only once outside (30: 6). It carries with it a solemn sense of doom, as indeed its first usage in 2 Kings 9: 25 suggests. The word occurs occasionally in other books (notably in Jer. 23: 33–8, translated 'burden'), but it is characteristic of Isa. 13–23. It may refer to a loud utterance (lifting up the voice) or to a raising of the hand to reinforce the spoken word of doom.

To most of these oracles precise dating cannot certainly be given. Some may well come from Isaiah himself. But others are clearly of a later date. Their ascription to Isaiah son of Amoz must therefore be due to the fact that the continuing body of Isaiah's disciples recognized them as in the Isaianic tradition. If, further, these later 'oracles' can be shown to be based on, and developing, an authentic Isaiah prophecy, they may have come from a prophet who was a member of the Isaiah community which persisted during and after the exile.

The underlying theme is that of God's active rule, to which all peoples, whether they know it or not, must be subject. In a sense, the temple hymns celebrating God's sovereignty imply this (Ps. 47), as do the coronation psalms (cp. Pss. 21, 72). But the practical implications were realized by the prophet and his disciples in history and experience as Israel was involved in world politics. Yet that realization came in a quite unexpected way. It was quite natural for a victorious nation to ascribe its victories as the extending of the sovereignty of the national god. The annals of Assyria, Babylon and Persia do this, and however pious the language, we could see this as an expression of national pride. The prophet of Israel makes this claim precisely when his people, and therefore its God, were defeated and discredited. The prophetic affirmation is one of a profound faith. Yet it can hardly be said to encourage or support national pride. For the same prophet has had to declare that historic Israel is quite unworthy to be the people of Yahweh, and moreover that their own humiliation is the work of their God. It is rather in spite of them, yet to recreate them, that their God is at work in history to manifest his active rule. The judgement on the nations is on account of their arrogance, cruelty and ruthless oppression of the weak. This is the faith that was to receive its finest expression in Isa. 40–55. ✳

THE JUDGEMENT ON BABYLON

BABYLON: AN ORACLE which Isaiah son of Amoz **13** received in a vision.

Raise the standard on a windy height,   2
roar out your summons,
beckon with arm upraised to the advance,

draw[a] your swords, you nobles.

3   I have given my warriors their orders
and summoned my fighting men to launch my anger;
they are eager for my triumph.

4   Hark, a tumult in the mountains, the sound of a vast
multitude;
hark, the roar of kingdoms, of nations gathering!
The LORD of Hosts is mustering a host for war,

5   men from a far country, from beyond the horizon.
It is the LORD with the weapons of his wrath
coming to lay the whole land waste.

6   Howl, for the Day of the LORD is at hand;
it comes, a mighty blow from Almighty God.

7   Thereat shall every hand hang limp,
every man's courage shall melt away,

8   his stomach hollow with fear;
anguish shall grip them, like a woman in labour.
One man shall look aghast at another,
and their faces shall burn with shame.

9   The Day of the LORD is coming indeed,
that cruel day of wrath and fury,
to make the land a desolation
and exterminate its wicked people.

10   The stars of heaven in their constellations shall give no
light,
the sun shall be darkened at its rising,
and the moon refuse to shine.

11   I will bring disaster upon the world
and their due punishment upon the wicked.
I will check the pride of the haughty

[a] draw: *so Sept.; Heb.* doors of.

and bring low the arrogance of ruthless men.
I will make men scarcer than fine gold,   12
rarer than gold of Ophir.
Then the heavens shall shudder,*a*   13
and the earth shall be shaken from its place
at the fury of the LORD of Hosts, on the day of his anger.

Then, like a gazelle before the hunter   14
or a flock with no man to round it up,
each man will go back to his own people,
every one will flee to his own land.

All who are found will be stabbed,   15
all who are taken will fall by the sword;
their infants will be dashed to the ground before their   16
        eyes,
their houses rifled and their wives ravished.

I will stir up against them the Medes,   17
who care nothing for silver and are not tempted by
        gold,*b*
who have no pity on little children   18
and spare no mother's son;
    and Babylon, fairest of kingdoms,   19
    proud beauty of the Chaldaeans,
shall be like Sodom and Gomorrah
    when God overthrew them.

    Never again shall she be inhabited,   20
no man shall dwell in her through all the ages;
there no Arab shall pitch his tent,
no shepherds fold their flocks.
There marmots shall have their lairs,   21

[a] *Prob. rdg.; Heb.* Then I will make the heavens shudder.
[b] *Prob. rdg.; Heb. adds* bows shall dash young men to the ground.

and porcupines[a] shall overrun her houses;
there desert owls shall dwell,
and there he-goats shall gambol;

22   jackals shall occupy her mansions,[b]
     and wolves her[c] gorgeous palaces.
Her time draws very near,
and her days have not long to run.

✻ In ch. 39 there is a prophecy that the Judaeans will be taken captive to Babylon because, contrary to Isaiah's advice, Hezekiah had joined forces with the Babylonian kingdom in revolt against their Assyrian overlord. In this section, however, Babylon is the world power, whose conquests have destroyed many kingdoms (14: 16f.). The historical situation is evidently that in which the empire is already threatened with attack along its northern borders (13: 17), or a little before 540 B.C. and so contemporary with chs. 40–55. Perhaps the verbal link with ch. 39 (Babylon) caused this section to be included in these oracles about foreign nations. It should however be observed that 13: 2–16 does not mention Babylon and is a poem about the day of God's victory, much of it, especially verses 6–13, in traditional terminology, cp. Zephaniah and Nahum. This may then be an older poem which could be applied on more than one occasion. It may have been originally applied to Assyria (against whom no 'oracle' is directed) and then re-applied to Babylon with the introduction of verse 1 and the addition of verses 17–22.

2. The last line in the Hebrew could be translated 'to enter the gates of the nobles' (cp. footnote). This could be a play on the name Babel which means 'the gate of the god'. If so the verse would refer to the Medo-Persian army, whom God

[a] *Mng. of Heb. word uncertain.*
[b] *Prob. rdg.; Heb.* her widows.
[c] *So Scroll; Heb. om.*

(not Cyrus) has commanded and consecrated for the fulfilment of his purpose (verses 3-5).

3. *warriors* is literally 'consecrated ones'. The army of Cyrus was in fact drawn from a number of nations.

10. The judgement is associated with cosmic disorder, as frequently in the prophets and in Mark 13: 24, so that darkness is universal before the new creation.

12. *gold of Ophir:* Ophir was in East Africa, but from Solomon's day (1 Kings 9: 28; 10: 11) the phrase became a popular expression for fine gold.

14. A description of panic flight.

15-16. A city invaded and mercilessly sacked.

17-22. It was the *Medes* who destroyed Nineveh, the capital of Assyria, in 612 B.C. and were included in Cyrus' army in 538 B.C. *Babylon* was not in fact destroyed, but made peaceful submission. It was still an inhabited city in the time of Alexander in 330 B.C. But the language, however revolting to us, is conventional and simply means that it will be conquered.

22. *mansions* for Hebrew 'widows' required only the change of one consonant, *l* to *r*, which in many languages are similar. ✻

RESTORATION

The LORD will show compassion for Jacob and will **14** once again make Israel his choice. He will settle them on their own soil, and strangers will come to join them and attach themselves to Jacob. Many*a* nations shall escort 2 Israel to her place, and she shall employ them as slaves and slave-girls on the land of the LORD; she shall take her captors captive and rule over her task-masters.

When the LORD gives you relief from your pain and 3 your fears and from the cruel slavery laid upon you,

[a] *So Scroll; Heb. om.*

4*a* you will take up this song of derision over the king of Babylon:

* A prose section, intended as a conclusion to the preceding poem, and closely resembling other passages in this book (49: 22f.; 56: 6–8; 60: 10, 14). The covenant relationship will be renewed, and Israel will fulfil her destiny to direct the nations to God (Exod. 19: 6).

4. This verse introduces the *song of derision*, for which the Hebrew word is commonly translated as proverb or parable. *derision-* or taunt-song is hardly adequate. As the word is used throughout the Bible it rather suggests holding up a mirror so that the human situation can be clearly seen, especially in the light of divine judgement and so lead men rightly to judge themselves. The English word *derision* emphasizes the emotions of the speaker; the Hebrew word emphasizes the intended effect on the hearer. *

THE OPPRESSOR IN THE UNDERWORLD

4*b*   See how the oppressor has met his end and his frenzy[a] ceased!

5   The LORD has broken the rod of the wicked,
         the sceptre of the ruler

6   who struck down peoples in his rage
             with unerring blows,
         who crushed nations in anger
         and persecuted them unceasingly.

7   The whole world has rest and is at peace;
         it breaks into cries of joy.

8   The pines themselves and the cedars of Lebanon exult
             over you:
         Since you have been laid low, they say,

[a] *So Scroll; Heb. word unknown.*

no man comes up to fell us.

Sheol below was all astir   9
   to meet you at your coming;
she roused the ancient dead to meet you,
   all who had been leaders on earth;
   she made all who had been kings of the nations
   rise from their thrones.

One and all they greet you with these words: 10
   So you too are weak as we are,
   and have become one of us!

Your pride and all the music of your lutes   11
   have been brought down to Sheol;[a]
maggots are the pallet beneath you,
   and worms your coverlet.

How you have fallen from heaven, bright morning star, 12
felled to the earth, sprawling helpless across the
   nations!

You thought in your own mind,   13
   I will scale the heavens;
I will set my throne high above the stars of God,
   I will sit on the mountain where the gods meet
   in the far recesses of the north.

I will rise high above the cloud-banks   14
   and make myself like the Most High.

Yet you shall be brought down to Sheol,   15
   to the depths of the abyss.

Those who see you will stare at you,   16
   they will look at you and ponder;

Is this, they will say, the man who shook the earth,

[a] *Or* Your pride has been brought down to Sheol to the crowding
throng of your dead.

who made kingdoms quake,

17   who turned the world into a desert
      and laid its cities in ruins,

who never let his prisoners go free to their homes,

18   the kings of every land?

Now they lie all of them in honour,
    each in his last home.

19   But you have been flung out unburied,
      mere loathsome carrion,*a*

a companion to the slain pierced by the sword
who have gone down to the stony abyss.

And you, a corpse trampled underfoot,

20   shall not share burial with them,

for you have ruined your land and slaughtered your
      people.

Such a brood of evildoers shall never be seen again.

21   Make the shambles ready for his sons
      butchered for their fathers' sin;

they shall not rise up and possess the world
nor cover the face of the earth with cities.

* The poem is addressed to the king of Babylon. It may
originally have been directed to Sargon II of Assyria who was
killed in battle in 705 B.C. and not buried in Assyria (cp. verse
19). The form of this poem is that of the funeral dirge introduced by the wailing word 'How!' The heavily accented
Hebrew words produce a 3:2 metre in each couplet, thus:

'who strúck down peóples in his ráge | with unérring blóws (6)

The effect is that of stumbling footsteps following the bier.
But instead of the wailing of the mourners, there are 'cries
of joy' (7), over the corpse of the oppressor. As he rests in

[*a*] carrion: *prob. rdg., cp. Sept.; Heb.* shoot.

peace, the whole world has rest and peace! Even the trees of Lebanon rejoice, since no more cedars will be cut down for the conqueror's palaces. In 9–11 the scene changes to Sheol, where the shades of the dead linger for a while before they fade away. There former kings, also mighty in their day, greet this great monarch mockingly as his pomp and glory come to the same pitiful end. The third section (verses 12–15) makes use of the language of myth. 'Bright morning star' represents two proper names of gods, Morning Star (Helel), Son of the Dawn (Shahar), minor deities in the pantheon of which El is the head. This godling thought to assert himself above all other gods and become equal with the Most High. Like a meteor, he will fall to the uttermost depths of Sheol. The fourth section (16–21) is deliberately longer than the first three, in order to bring out the point of the parable. First the mourners recognize that the king, hitherto greeted with the salutation 'O King, live for ever!', was mortal. He reigned supreme, feared by all, but in death suffered the supreme shame of an unburied corpse while even the conquered kings were honourably buried by their people. For his imperialist policies have brought ruin upon his own people. In spite of its unfamiliar language, the parable is disturbingly modern.

The past tense of the poem is deliberate, as if to say 'It has virtually happened already because God has decided it.'

9. *Sheol* is the Hebrew name for the underworld to which the dead go. There they continue for a while a kind of shadowy existence away from the interests of God or man (cp. Ps. 88: 5, 10–12).

13. *mountain:* the Ras Shamra texts (discovered in the scribal library of the Canaanite city of Ugarit – see *The Making of the Old Testament,* pp. 25ff. in this series) refer to this home of the gods, comparable to the Greek Mount Olympus (cp. Ezek. 28: 14).

19. *stony abyss:* the exact significance of this phrase is obscure. It must be linked with 'depths of the abyss' in verse 15 and may refer to the common grave on the battlefield into which

the dead were thrown and covered with stones in order to save the corpses from mutilation by jackals.

21. *with cities* hardly seems appropriate here. The Hebrew word may, with the alteration of one letter, be read as 'ruins'. ✶

THE END OF BABYLON

22   I will rise against them, says the LORD of Hosts; I will destroy the name of Babylon and what remains of her,

23 her offspring and posterity, says the LORD; I will make her a haunt of the bustard, a waste of fen, and sweep her with the besom of destruction. This is the very word of the LORD of Hosts.

✶ A prose addition, apparently by the author of verses 1–4*a*, applying the poem to the end of the Babylonian Empire. It is similar to 13: 20–2. ✶

THE ASSYRIAN INVADER SHALL
BE DESTROYED

24   The LORD of Hosts has sworn:
In very truth, as I planned, so shall it be;*a*
as I designed, so shall it fall out:

25   I will break the Assyrian in my own land
and trample him underfoot upon my mountains;
his yoke shall be lifted from you,
his burden taken from your*b* shoulders.

26   This is the plan prepared for the whole earth,
this the hand stretched out over all the nations.

[*a*] *So Scroll; Heb.* so it was.
[*b*] from you...your: *so Scroll; Heb.* from them...their.

> For the LORD of Hosts has prepared his plan: 27
> > who shall frustrate it?
> His is the hand stretched out, and who shall turn it back?

✳ This passage brings us back to the eighth-century Isaiah and the invasion of Sennacherib. The defeat of *the Assyrian* will bring relief to Judah, and then to the whole world which Assyria had conquered. This is God's purpose and cannot be prevented. ✳

A WARNING FOR PHILISTIA

In the year that King Ahaz died this oracle came from   28
God:

> Let none of you rejoice, you Philistines,   29
> > because the rod that chastised you is broken;
> for a viper shall be born of a snake as a plant from the
> > root,
> > and its fruit shall be a flying serpent.
> But the poor shall graze their flocks in my meadows,   30
> > and the destitute shall lie down in peace;
> > but the offspring of your roots I will kill by starvation,
> > > and put[a] the remnant of you to death.
> Howl in the gate, cry for help in the city,   31
> > let all Philistia be in turmoil;
> > for a great enemy is coming from the north,
> > > not a man straying from[b] his ranks.
> What anwser is there for the envoys of the nation?   32
> This, that the LORD has fixed Zion in her place,
> and the afflicted among his people shall take refuge
> > there.

[a] *So Scroll; Heb.* and he will put.
[b] *So Scroll; Heb.* no one alone in...

✶ While the main theme is clear, viz. a warning against premature rejoicing over the death of the oppressor, the details are obscure. It is precisely dated in verse 28, presumably 715 B.C. But Ahaz cannot be the 'rod that chastised', cp. 2 Chron. 28: 18. This must be the Assyrian king, presumably Tiglath-pileser III (died 727), Shalmaneser V (died 722) or Sargon II (died 705). The death of any of these kings might have provoked expectations of relief, and in fact the general revolt of vassals, including Judah, Ashkelon and Ekron, did break out at the death of Sargon II. But the date of Ahaz' death does not correspond to the death of any of the Assyrian kings. It may be that what is referred to is the false expectation of Sargon's defeat by the Egyptians suggested in Isa. 20, which led Ashdod to revolt in 713 and almost involved Hezekiah of Judah. This brought a terrible vengeance on Ashdod in 711, when Sargon besieged the city and then conquered it.

29. *a viper...*: a proverbial saying, meaning that things will go from bad to worse.

30*b* describes the siege and eventual conquest of the city. It is possible that 30*a* should follow verse 32.

32. The *answer* is as much an answer to the Judaean king as to the Philistine envoys, and an answer which at the last moment Hezekiah heeded, on this occasion. ✶

LAMENT OVER THE DESTRUCTION OF MOAB

✶ In this section there appear to be two laments, 15: 1–9 and 16: 6–12, an appeal for help 16: 1, 3–5 (16: 2 should possibly follow 15: 9), and a prophecy of doom for the Moabites (16: 13f.). According to 16: 13, what precedes was spoken 'long ago', although the Hebrew does not necessarily mean the remote past. It should be noted that a number of verses in these chapters are also found in Jer. 48: 29–38, although in a different order. These verses are 15: 2–7; 16: 6–12. If 16: 13f. is from Isaiah, then what precedes could refer to the time of Jeroboam II (2 Kings 14: 25) although the language would be exaggerated. It would better suit the historical situation in 650 B.C., when the land of Moab was invaded by Arabian tribes, and its political integrity destroyed. This too would account for the number of place-names referred to. These verses then would be the words of an unknown seventh-century prophet.

The territory of Moab lay east of the Dead Sea; its northern border was the Arnon river, its southern the gorge of the Arabim (Isa. 15: 7) whose waters flow into the southern end of the Dead Sea. The relationship between the Israelites and Moabites was usually hostile from the time of the settlement (Judg. 3: 12–29) and this is referred to in Pss. 60: 8; 83: 6 as well as by various prophets. The territory was conquered by David and became part of his empire, and also formed part of the empire of Omri. During the reign of Jehoram, Moab successfully rebelled (2 Kings 3: 27), and became independent, a fact which is more fully reported on the Moabite Stone. (For an account of the Stone see *The Making of the Old Testament*, pp. 29–32.) This hostility is reflected in the scandalous story of the origin of the Moabites in Gen. 19: 30–8. But the story also reflects a sense of common kinship; David was able to leave members of his family in the safety of the Moabite court (1 Sam. 22: 3f.), and the story of Ruth reflects the same spirit. It is this which comes to expression in the laments of this section, as it does in the appeal for help by the Moabites to Jerusalem. Their doom is certain, but the prophet is deeply distressed on their account (15: 5; 16: 9). ✵

Moab: an oracle.   15

On the night when Ar is sacked, Moab meets her doom;
on the night when Kir is sacked, Moab meets her doom.
The people of Dibon go up[a] to the hill-shrines to weep; 2
Moab howls over Nebo and over Medeba.

[a] The people...go up: *Prob. ridg.; Heb.* He has gone up to the house and Dibon.

The hair is torn from every head, and every beard
    shaved off.

3   In the streets men go clothed with sackcloth,
        they cry out[a] on the roofs;
    in the public squares every man howls,
        weeping as he goes through them.

4   Heshbon and Elealeh cry for help,
    their voices are heard as far as Jahaz.
    Thus Moab's stoutest warriors become cowards,
    and her courage ebbs away.

5   My heart cries out for Moab,
    whose nobles have fled[b] as far as Zoar.[c]
On the ascent to Luhith men go up weeping;
on the road to Horonaim there are cries of[d] 'Disaster!'

6   The waters of Nimrim are desolate indeed;
the grass is parched, the herbage dead,
        not a green thing is left;

7   and so the people carry off across the gorge of the
        Arabim
    their hard-earned wealth and all their savings.

8   The cry for help echoes round the frontiers of Moab,
their howling reaches Eglaim and Beer-elim.

9   The waters of Dimon already run with blood;
    yet I have more troubles in store for Dimon,
        for I have a vision[e] of the survivors of Moab,
        of the remnant of Admah.

[a] they cry out: *prob. rdg.*, *cp. Sept.; Heb. om.*
[b] have fled: *prob. rdg.; Heb. om.*
[c] *Prob. rdg.; Heb. adds* Eglath Shelishiya.
[d] there are cries of: *prob. rdg., cp. Vulg.; Heb. unintelligible.*
[e] I have a vision: *prob. rdg.; Heb.* a lion.

the daughters of Moab at the fords of the Arnon   **16**₂
shall be like fluttering birds, like scattered nestlings.

✳ The first lament over the catastrophe that has befallen
Moab. The form of the poem is in the traditional 3:2 measure
appropriate to a funeral dirge (cp. 14: 4*b*–21). The movement
geographically is from south to north in Moabite territory,
from the southern border with Edom to the northern with
Ammon. The plight of the refugees is described as they seek
refuge in Edom carrying what possessions they can rescue.
The mention of Zoar in verse 5 may be a deliberate reminder
of the flight of Lot, the ancestor of the Moabites (Gen. 19:
22, 23).

2–3. These verses describe the traditional mourning practices.

8. The news of the catastrophe spreads to Ammonite
territory. ✳

AN APPEAL FOR HELP

The rulers of the country send a present of lambs   1
    from Sela in the wilderness
  to the hill of the daughter of Zion.
'Take up our cause with all your might;   3
let your shadow shield us at high noon, dark as night.
Shelter the homeless, do not betray the fugitive;   4
let the homeless people of Moab find refuge with you;
hide them from the despoiler.'

When extortion has done its work and the looting is
    over,
  when the heel of the oppressor has vanished from
    the land,
a throne shall be set up in mutual trust in David's tent,   5
  and on it there shall sit a true judge,
one who seeks justice and is swift to do right.

✷ Apparently some Moabite refugees in Edom sent to Jerusalem the traditional tribute (cp. 2 Kings 3 : 4) as if to acknowledge that Moab was a vassal state of Judah and so to claim
protection. They asked to be allowed to enter Judaean territory
and live there under Judaean protection. This would be the
beginning of a restoration to conditions as they were under
David. If this appeal came from the Moabites, it indicates that
they knew something of hopes associated with the Davidic
dynasty (cp. Ps. 89: 19–37) and with the language of the
coronation hymns (cp. Isa. 11: 3f.). This is quite possible since
Moabite ambassadors would be present at the investiture of a
Judaean king. In the circumstances of the seventh century, or
any period after Solomon, this may be flattery, but it is a
subtle form of flattery which could hardly fail to appeal to
the hearers. If this took place about 650 B.C., it would be
tempting to find here an explanation of the event recorded in
2 Chron. 33: 11, for such action would seem to the Assyrian
colonial office an independence that could not be tolerated. ✷

SECOND LAMENT OVER MOAB

6   We have heard tell of Moab's pride, how great it is,
       we have heard of his pride, his overweening pride;
            his talk is full of lies.
7   For this all Moab shall howl;
       Moab shall howl indeed;
     he*a* shall mourn for the prosperous farmers of Kir-
            hareseth,
            utterly ruined;
8   the orchards of Heshbon,
            the vines of Sibmah languish,
     though their red grapes once laid low the lords of the
            nations,

[a] *Prob. rdg.; Heb.* you.

though they reached as far as Jazer
and trailed out to the wilderness,
though their branches spread abroad and crossed the sea.
Therefore I will weep for Sibmah's vines as I weep for 9
Jazer.
I will drench you with my tears, Heshbon and Elealeh;
for over your summer-fruits and your harvest
the shouts of the harvesters are ended.
Joy and gladness shall be banished from the meadows, 10
no more shall men shout and sing in the vineyards,
no more shall they tread wine in the winepresses;
I have silenced the shouting of the harvesters.
Therefore my heart throbs   11
like a harp for Moab,
and my very soul for Kir-hareseth.*a*
When Moab comes to worship   12
and wearies himself at the hill-shrines,
when he enters his sanctuary to pray,
he will gain nothing.

* This hardly sounds like a response to the appeal for help
in the previous verses, unless 'his talk is full of lies' (6) is
meant to dismiss verse 5 as insincere flattery. It is best to regard
the poem as a lament unconnected with the appeal for help.
Again the tone is that of genuine sympathy and grief for
Moab's suffering (9, 11). Yet this does not blind the prophet
to the fact that 'overweening pride' (6) is the cause of Moab's
humiliation.

7. *prosperous farmers:* the word, though rare, is usually
translated as 'raisin-cakes' (cp. Hos. 3: 1 and the Revised
Standard Version here; also 2 Sam. 6: 19). On the other hand
Jer. 48: 31 has 'men' (the Hebrew word is somewhat similar);

[a] *Prob. rdg.; Heb.* Kir-hares.

again it is not certain whether *utterly ruined* refers to the *farmers* or the mourners (see the Revised Standard Version for an alternative translation of verses 7, 8). Raisin-cakes were used in the religious festivals and these have come to an end.

9–10. These verses describe the ruin caused by the invaders at harvest time.

11. *my heart throbs:* the Hebrew uses words to describe the physical effects of emotion, throbbing like a harp string. ✶

THE DOOM OF MOAB

13 These are the words which the LORD spoke long ago
14 about Moab; and now he says, In three years, as a hired labourer counts them off, the glory of Moab shall become contemptible for all his vast numbers; a handful shall be left[a] and those of no account.

✶ An application of the laments to a new situation in which Moab is about to come to a complete end.

14. *In three years* refers to some kind of contract for which a labourer hired himself to work for another. He would carefully note the time, eagerly waiting for his release. We might paraphrase 'In precisely three years'. ✶

ORACLE AGAINST DAMASCUS AND EPHRAIM

17　　　　　　Damascus: an oracle.

Damascus shall be a city no longer,
　　she shall be but a heap of ruins.
2　For ever desolate, flocks shall have her for their own,[b]
　　and lie there undisturbed.
3　　No longer shall Ephraim boast a fortified city,

[a] shall be left: *so Sept.; Heb.* a remnant.
[b] For ever...own: *so Sept.; Heb.* The cities of Aroer shall be deserted for flocks.

or Damascus a kingdom;
the remnant of Aram and the glory of Israel, their fate
    is one.
This is the very word of the LORD of Hosts.

On that day Jacob's weight shall dwindle   4
    and the fat on his limbs waste away,
as when the harvester gathers up the standing corn,   5
    and reaps the ears in armfuls,
or as when a man gleans the ears in the Vale of Rephaim,
    or as when one beats an olive-tree   6
and only gleanings are left on it,
two or three berries on the top of a branch,
    four or five on the boughs of the fruiting tree.
This is the very word of the LORD the God of Israel.

✳ The title refers only to Damascus but the oracles refer also
to Ephraim. Although the title is attached to the whole
chapter, it applies only to the first six verses. The remainder
consist of oracles or fragments of oracles of uncertain date.
The verses clearly refer to the Assyrian invasion which resulted
in the capture of Damascus and the loss of most of Israelite
territory in 732 B.C.

3. *No longer shall Ephraim boast a fortified city* suggests that
the terms imposed by Tiglath-pileser on Israel was the destruction of the defences of Samaria. If so, they were restored by
Hoshea when he rebelled.

4–6. This vividly represents the reduction of the northern
kingdom from its former glory under Jeroboam II to its pitiful
proportions under Hoshea (cp. 2 Kings 15: 29–30). The simile
is drawn from a scene familiar to a Judaean, of a harvest in
the Vale of Rephaim, south-west of Jerusalem. It meant the
end of the Aramaean kingdom of Damascus and the reduction
of Ephraim to insignificance. ✳

TURN TO THE LORD FROM IDOLS

7 On that day men shall look to their Maker and turn
8 their eyes to the Holy One of Israel; they shall not look
to the altars made by their own hands nor to anything
that their fingers have made, sacred poles or incense-altars.

✴ 7. *On that day* does not connect with the preceding oracle
but is a fragment of some longer oracle. It resembles 2: 20,
and the actual word for *men* occurs four times in ch. 2.
Whether this is a fragment of one of Isaiah's oracles or a
reflection of some of his disciples, is uncertain. Certainly it
reflects Isaiah's teaching, and its theme derives from Exod.
20: 4f.

8. *sacred poles* were symbolic representations of the Canaanite
mother goddess. ✴

THE RESULTS OF IDOLATRY

9 On that day their strong cities shall be deserted like the
cities of the Hivites and the Amorites,[a] which they
abandoned when Israel came in; all shall be desolate.

10   For you forgot the God who delivered you,
                and did not remember the rock, your stronghold.
           Plant then, if you will, your gardens in honour of Adonis,
                strike your cuttings for a foreign god;
11   protect your gardens on the day you plant them,
                and next day make the seed sprout.
           But the crop will be scorched when wasting disease
                comes
                in the day of incurable pain.

[a] Hivites...Amorites: *prob. rdg.*, *cp. Sept.*; *Heb.* woodland and hill-
country.

✶ This passage may be compared with 1: 29–31. The context in which the oracle appears suggests that it was directed against the northern kingdom, and the fertility rites referred to at Hos. 4: 13 would support this. But 2 Kings 16: 4 speaks of fertility rites in Judah under Ahaz.

9. We should perhaps read 'your' *strong cities* with the Septuagint.

10. *Adonis* represents a word which in earlier versions was understood as 'pleasant'. It was a name given in Phoenicia to the god Tammuz (Ezek. 8: 14), whom the Greeks called Adonis, a Semitic word meaning 'My Lord'. The cult of Adonis was known in Greece from the time of Plato. The practices referred to here are those associated with the cult of Adonis who annually died and rose again in a myth, symbolizing the death and rebirth of vegetation. Seeds which quickly germinated and cuttings whose growth could be stimulated were used to represent or even hasten this resurrection. Of course such forced growth had no permanence, but in the cultic act this was of no importance. The prophet insists that a religion of this kind cannot meet man's needs in his hour of trial. He would recall his people to the God who was their *rock* and *stronghold*, who had *delivered* from oppression. Why pin hope on what can only wither, and abandon him who alone can save? ✶

THE ROARING OF THE NATIONS

Listen! it is the thunder of many peoples,   12
they thunder with the thunder of the sea.
Listen! it is the roar of nations
roaring with the roar of mighty waters.*   13
When he rebukes them, away they fly,
driven like chaff on the hills before the wind,
   like thistledown before the storm.

[a] *So some MSS.; others add* peoples roar with the roar of great waters.

14   At evening all is confusion,
            and before morning they are gone.
        Such is the fate of our plunderers,
            the lot of those who despoil us.

* Although Assyria is not specifically named, it is reasonable to connect this oracle with the invasion in 701 B.C. of Sennacherib, whose army included soldiers from various parts of his empire. Some commentators, however, would see these verses as the work of a post-exilic prophet and as expressing his expectation of the End-time, as in Joel 2. In the mind of the hearers, the language of verse 12 would certainly evoke the portrayal in the Semitic creation-myth of the terrible chaos-monster, Tiamat, and her attendant brood. But they are dismissed with almost laughable ease by Yahweh. So will it be with the terrible foe threatening destruction. *

A MESSAGE FOR EGYPT

* This unusually phrased passage can best be understood against the background of events immediately preceding 711 B.C. when a coalition of small Syrian states rebelled against their Assyrian overlord, Sargon II (cp. Isa. 20). This revolt was instigated by Egypt whose policy was to resist the threat of invasion to the last Syrian – including Judah. Hezekiah was in fact involved in the early stages but withdrew before the final stages of the rebellion, as it would appear from the Assyrian records. He appears to have heeded the warnings of Isaiah on this occasion.

Egypt during the middle of the eighth century had been weakened by a series of civil wars. In 715, the Ethiopian Piankhi made himself master of all Egypt and began the Twenty-Fifth Dynasty. Under him and his successors Egypt regained for a time something of its earlier position as a great power, and prepared to resist the encroachments of the Mesopotamian

power into Syria and Egypt itself. To this end envoys from
Egypt were sent to the Syrian states assuring them of Egyptian
support; they in turn, who were suffering under the oppressive rule and heavy taxation of Assyria, were eager to gain
Egyptian aid.

Consistently with his prophetic faith, Isaiah rejected any
kind of alliance. He saw the whole course of events as firmly
under God's control. An alliance with a foreign power was
not only useless, but a betrayal of the alliance (the covenant)
with Judah's true overlord, Yahweh. He will take action in
his own time, and until the signal is given any activity is
premature and disastrous. Events in 711 B.C. and later in
701 were to demonstrate the truth of Isaiah's teaching. Assyria
will be overcome in God's own time and not before. Again,
as in 14: 26, Isaiah declares his message not for Judah alone,
but for the whole world. ✳

There is a land of sailing ships,   **18**
    a land beyond the rivers of Cush
    which sends its envoys by the Nile,[a]   2
journeying on the waters in vessels of reed.
Go, swift messengers,
    go to a people tall and smooth-skinned,
    to a people dreaded near and far,
    a nation strong and proud,
    whose land is scoured by rivers.
All you who dwell in the world, inhabitants of earth,   3
shall see when the signal is hoisted on the mountains
    and shall hear when the trumpet sounds.

These were the words of the LORD to me: 4

    From my dwelling-place I will look quietly down

[a] *Lit.* sea.

when the heat shimmers in the summer sun,
when the dew is heavy at harvest time.[a]

5 Before the vintage, when the budding is over
and the flower ripens into a berry,
the shoots shall be cut down with knives,
the branches struck off and cleared away.

6 All shall be left to birds of prey on the hills
and to beasts of the earth;
in summer the birds shall make their home there,
in winter every beast of the earth.

7 At that time tribute shall be brought to the LORD of
Hosts from[b] a people tall and smooth-skinned, dreaded
near and far, a nation strong and proud, whose land is
scoured by rivers. They shall bring it to Mount Zion, the
place where men invoke the name of the LORD of Hosts.

✷ Ch. 18 may be divided into three sections: verses 1–3, a
reply to the Egyptian envoys; verses 4–6, a private oracle to
the prophet; verse 7, postscript.

1. *sailing ships:* earlier renderings had 'whirring wings' and
understood this as a reference to the winged insects of the
Nile. The N.E.B. understands this, literally, as winged ships,
i.e. boats with sails. *Cush*, i.e. Ethiopia.

2. *vessels of reed* were constructed of papyrus made water-
tight with bitumen. Recent attempts to construct such vessels
have shown that while difficulties might be experienced in
severe storms, they were easily navigable. *tall and smooth skinned*
well describes the Nubians by contrast with the Judaeans.
Herodotus describes them as the 'tallest and most beautiful of
men'. The language of this verse is in the style of diplomacy,
and, since he was a recognized prophet, may well be Isaiah's
message to the envoys, given in response to Hezekiah's request

[a] time: *so Sept.; Heb.* heat.   [b] from: *so Scroll; Heb. om.*

for guidance. But the actual message to be returned in verse 3 is not for Egypt alone; it is for all mankind.

It shoud be noted that this section is, in Hebrew, introduced by an exclamation 'Woe', not represented in the N.E.B. The word usually introduces an oracle of doom or a lament (cp. 1: 4, 24; 10: 5 etc.), and may indicate that Isaiah already has a premonition that the new power of Egypt will be short-lived.

4–6 provide the private oracle which prompted the words of 2f. It is a vision of God quietly and unhurriedly ruling over all human affairs, even those of the great powers. As certainly as the year moves towards its end (harvest-time) so he will act in judgement and bring to an end (a harvest of destruction) the power of Assyria. It may also be a deliberately cryptic oracle: a great power is to be destroyed, it could be either Assyria or Egypt. Let Egypt beware lest its ambitions prove self-destructive.

7. The verse is in prose and may be a later reflection based on verse 2 and similar to 45: 14. It could be understood as the comment of a post-exilic disciple of the Isaianic community who linked together these two passages, and associated them with the rebuilt temple. ✶

EGYPT'S DOOM

Egypt: an oracle.   **19**

See how the LORD comes riding swiftly upon a cloud,
 he shall descend upon Egypt;
 the idols of Egypt quail before him,
 Egypt's courage melts within her.
 I will set Egyptian against Egyptian,   2
 and they shall fight one against another,
  neighbour against neighbour,
city against city and kingdom against kingdom.

3   Egypt's spirit shall sink within her,
        and I will throw her counsels into confusion.
     They may resort to idols and oracle-mongers,
        to ghosts and spirits,
4   but I will hand Egypt over to a hard master,
     and a cruel king shall rule over them.
     This is the very word of the Lord, the LORD of Hosts.

5   The waters of the Nile[a] shall drain away,
     the river shall be parched and run dry;
6   its channels shall stink,
   the streams of Egypt shall be parched and dry up;
     reeds and rushes shall wither away;
7   the lotus too beside the Nile[b]
     and all that is sown along the Nile shall dry up,
        shall be blown away and vanish.
8   The fishermen shall groan and lament,
     all who cast their hooks into the Nile
   and those who spread nets on the water shall lose heart.
9   The flax-dressers shall hang their heads,
     the women carding and the weavers shall grow pale,[c]
10   Egypt's spinners shall be downcast,
     and all her artisans sick at heart.

11   Fools that you are, you princes of Zoan!
   Wisest of Pharaoh's counsellors you may be,
     but stupid counsellors you are.
     How can you say to Pharaoh,
   'I am the heir of wise men and spring from ancient
       kings'?

[a] *Lit.* sea. [b] *Prob. rdg.; Heb. adds* on the mouth of the Nile.
[c] shall grow pale: *so Scroll; Heb.* white linen.

Where are your wise men, Pharaoh,   12
to teach you and make known to you
what the LORD of Hosts has planned for Egypt?
Zoan's princes are fools, the princes of Noph are dupes;   13
the chieftains of her clans have led Egypt astray.
The LORD has infused into them*a*   14
a spirit that warps their judgement;
they make Egypt miss her way in all she does,
as a drunkard will miss his footing as he vomits.
There shall be nothing in Egypt that any man can do,   15
head or tail, palm or rush.

✶ The three oracles, 1–4, 5–10, 11–15, and indeed the remainder of the chapter all refer to Egypt, and that is the reason for their being gathered together, to follow ch. 18 and precede ch. 20. It is very doubtful whether there is any continuity from one to another, and the historical setting is difficult to determine. These verses could be associated with the civil wars that preceded the establishment of the Twenty-Fifth Dynasty under Piankhi in 715 (cp. verses 2, 4), with the conquest of part of Egypt by Assyria in the following century by Esar-haddon or Ashur-bani-pal, or conquest by the Babylonians or Persians in the sixth century. The allusions in these verses are not sufficiently clear to determine the date. The connecting theme is the doom of Egypt.

1–4. Political and social confusion.

1. *See* represents a Hebrew exclamation frequently in prophetic oracles introducing a threat (3: 1 (N.E.B. 'be warned'); 24: 1 (N.E.B. 'Beware'); 30: 27). God is described, in the language of an ancient myth known in the Ras Shamra tablets and used in Pss. 18: 10; 104: 3, as coming for judgement (cp. Nahum 1: 3). *Egypt* appears seven times in these four verses as though by sheer repetition to nail down the judgement.

[*a*] *So Sept.; Heb.* her.

3. *They may resort....:* A familiar picture for 'loss of nerve'. In the best form of Egyptian religion there was a confidence in the right ordering of the world (*ma'at*). When this failed there was a frantic resort to divination.

4. *a hard master:* either an indigenous strong ruler or a foreign conqueror.

5–10. The drying-up of the Nile. The whole economy of Egypt, where rain was practically unknown, was dependent on the annual flooding of the Nile, which brought not only water but also rich alluvial soil from its upper reaches. If for any reason this should fail, the whole food-supply would fail. It was only in reasonable proximity to the Nile that life could go on. If its waters dried up, the desert sands would soon engulf towns and villages.

5. *the Nile* in this verse is literally 'the sea' (see footnote *a*), by which is meant the mysterious underground sea from which rivers and springs came.

11–15. The failure of Egyptian wisdom. The wisdom of Egypt was highly regarded in the ancient world, and the wise men played an important role in the affairs of government. They were careful to conserve the sayings of earlier sages through the centuries and many of these documents have been found. Much of Israel's wisdom literature goes back to that of Egypt, introduced apparently by Solomon (cp. R. N. Whybray, *Proverbs*, in this series). In this poem, these wise men have failed to discern the signs of the times, and particularly the supremacy of God (verse 12). Inevitably, therefore, their judgement was warped; they are 'fools' and 'dupes' (13). The failure of wisdom is as disastrous politically as is that of the Nile water economically.

13. *Zoan* (Tanis) and *Noph* (Memphis) were two cities that were at various times the seat of government in Egypt.

15. *head or tail, palm or rush.* The closing words are part of a wisdom saying or popular proverb, as we might say: 'king and commoner, oak and ivy'; cp. 9: 14. ✴

FIVE ORACLES IN PROSE

When that day comes the Egyptians shall become weak 16
as women; they shall fear and tremble when they see the
LORD of Hosts raise his hand against them, as raise it he
will. The land of Judah shall strike terror into Egypt; its 17
very name shall cause dismay, because of the plans that
the LORD of Hosts has laid against them.

When that day comes there shall be five cities in Egypt 18
speaking the language of Canaan and swearing allegiance
to the LORD of Hosts, and one of them shall be called the
City of the Sun.[a]

When that day comes there shall be an altar to the 19
LORD in the heart of Egypt, and a sacred pillar set up for
the LORD upon her frontier. It shall stand as a token and a 20
reminder to the LORD of Hosts in Egypt, so that when they
appeal to him against their oppressors, he may send a
deliverer to champion their cause, and he shall rescue
them. The LORD will make himself known to the Egyp- 21
tians; on that day they shall acknowledge the LORD and
do him service with sacrifice and grain-offering, make
vows to him and pay them. The LORD will strike down 22
Egypt, healing as he strikes;[b] then they will turn back to
him and he will hear their prayers and heal them.

When that day comes there shall be a highway between 23
Egypt and Assyria; Assyrians shall come to Egypt and
Egyptians to Assyria; then Egyptians shall worship with[c]
Assyrians.

[a] the City of the Sun: *or* Heliopolis; *so some MSS.; others* the city of
destruction.
[b] healing as he strikes: *so Heb.; Scroll has* striking until their resistance
is broken.   [c] *Or* shall be slaves to.

24 When that day comes Israel shall rank with Egypt and
Assyria, those three, and shall be a blessing in the centre
25 of the world. So the LORD of Hosts will bless them: A
blessing be upon Egypt my people, upon Assyria the
work of my hands, and upon Israel my possession.

✶ These five oracles, each introduced by *When that day comes*,
have been added to verses 1–15 by the compiler of the book.
There is an obvious progression of thought from hostility to
Egypt to a quite extraordinary vision of the whole world
(Egypt and Assyria), united as the people of God. The oracles
could be seen as a series of footnotes, attached to the preceding
verses by Isaiah's disciples as their own understanding of the
divine purpose declared in 2: 2–4 was deepened. Indeed the
fifth oracle (24–5) is probably the most remarkable in the
Old Testament in its expression of universalism, a fine interpretation of the blessing of Abraham in Gen. 12: 3 or of
Jacob in Gen. 28: 14. Israel's true function as a 'kingdom of
priests' (Exod. 19: 5–6) is here fulfilled.

Any attempt to date these prophecies must be tentative.
They have been assigned to various periods from the eighth
to the third centuries B.C. Much will depend upon the understanding of 'Assyria' in verses 23–5. Does this refer to the
historic Assyria of the eighth and seventh centuries, or is it a
symbolic term for the traditional enemy of Israel? What are
the 'five cities in Egypt...swearing allegiance to the LORD'
and the 'City of the Sun' in verse 18? Does the altar of verse 19
refer to that erected by a Jewish colony in Elephantiné at the
first cataract of the Nile in the fifth century? We would suggest
that a post-exilic date without further precision would best
suit both style and contents of these verses. They must certainly be earlier than 200 B.C. since they are included in the
Qumran Isaiah scroll.

16f. *Judah shall strike terror into Egypt:* there is no suggestion
that Judah will conquer Egypt. The fear is brought about by

the fulfilment of God's purpose. This seems to allude to verse 12.

raise his hand: while the word for *raise* is most commonly used as a cultic term (cp. Exod. 29: 26, 'special gift') its meaning here seems to be a threatening gesture.

18. *five cities in Egypt . . . swearing allegiance to the LORD:* this may be an allusion to Josh. 10: 5, and so meant to suggest a new invasion leading to the conversion of Egypt. *the language of Canaan:* i.e. Hebrew, as the proper language of worship (cp. Zeph. 3: 9). *the City of the Sun* suggests the Greek name Heliopolis (see footnote *a*), for the Egyptian 'House of the Sun' (Jer. 43: 13, 'Beth-Shemesh' – i.e. House of the Sun). The alternative reading 'destruction' translates a similar Hebrew word in many manuscripts representing later Jewish hostility. In Jer. 44: 1, four cities are mentioned in which Jews sought refuge during Babylonian occupation. This prophet has added a fifth.

19–22. This passage may be associated with Zech. 14: 16–19, but the language is strange. It is remarkable that *an altar*, and presumably therefore a temple, outside Jerusalem should be approved. It is even more remarkable that a *sacred pillar* (*masṣebah*) designated as *for the LORD* should be approved. It may be that the prophet sees here a renewal of the patriarchal period (cp. Gen. 35: 7; 28: 18), but now in Egypt. Egypt is now to have its patriarchal period as Israel had. This will be its Beth-El. In the next sentence *Egypt* will experience its release from slavery (cp. Exod. 20: 1) and find a deliverer to *champion* its *cause* (cp. Judg. 3: 9 etc.). Then Egypt will be able to offer worship to God according to the torah. And if God has to *strike down* Egypt as he had struck Israel, it will be in order that he may heal (cp. Hos. 6: 1). The prophet thus describes Egypt as experiencing the same discipline as had Israel, the people of God.

23. A great *highway* will link together the rival powers of the ancient world. This will no longer be merely the trade-route, and not at all the military road along which the hostile

armies went. It will be the Pilgrim's way (cp. Ps. 84: 5), where all rivalry and barriers will disappear.

24–5. The climax. Israel together with its ancient oppressor *Egypt*, and its cruel conqueror Assyria (or any Mesopotamian empire) will become the people of God. This will be a new kind of confederacy, not merely of the tribes that formed Israel, but of the peoples of the world. Each of the phrases, *my people, the work of my hands, my possession*, is peculiarly associated with Israel throughout the Old Testament. The divine blessing, the sole source of the life of God's people, will permeate the whole world of mankind, united in the worship of Yahweh, the living God. The Christian will see this as an essential part of the New Testament hope, finely expressed in Rev. 7: 9–10; 15: 3–4. ✶

THE CAPTIVES' CLOTHING

20 Sargon king of Assyria sent his commander-in-chief[a] to
2 Ashdod, and he took it by storm. At that time the LORD said to[b] Isaiah son of Amoz, Come, strip the sackcloth from your waist and take your sandals off. He did so,
3 and went about naked and barefoot. The LORD said, My servant Isaiah has gone naked and barefoot for three years
4 as a sign and a warning to Egypt and Cush; just so shall the king of Assyria lead the captives of Egypt and the exiles of Cush naked and barefoot, their buttocks shame-
5 fully exposed, young and old alike. All men shall be dismayed, their hopes in Cush and their pride in Egypt
6 humbled. On that day those who dwell along this coast will say, So much for all our hopes on which we relied[c] for help and deliverance from the king of Assyria; what escape have we now?

[a] *Or* sent Tartan.   [b] *So Sept.; Heb.* through.
[c] *So Scroll; Heb.* to which we fled.

✶ This chapter contains a biographical note by one of Isaiah's disciples of a divine command received by the prophet. It occurred when a number of small kingdoms, especially that of Ashdod, at the instigation of Egypt, had rebelled against Assyria in 714 B.C. The revolt was in fact crushed by Sargon II and Ashdod was savagely punished. Judah took part in the initial stages but, warned by Isaiah, withdrew and escaped Ashdod's fate (cp. 14: 28–32; 18: 1–6). But the prophet looked beyond this to the eventual conquest of Egypt under the Ethiopian ('Cush') dynasty.

The 'sign and warning' (verse 3) was seen by all, to prompt the question: 'What does this mean?' Its meaning was told by Isaiah to his disciples. Obviously this sign was not merely for Ashdod, still less for Egypt. It was intended as a warning for the Judaean king not to join the revolt lest Judah suffer a like fate. We should regard this prophetic action as similar to the naming of his sons in 7: 3 and 8: 1ff. It is a symbolic act, performed at God's command and therefore full of divine energy to bring about that which it symbolized. It brought into history the events which it portrayed in action, the capture and exile of Ashdod and Egypt. It is not a magical action performed to bring about man's wishes. It is divinely ordered, and the medium of divine revelation.

1. *Sargon* ruled 722–705 B.C. The capture of *Ashdod* is described on one of his inscriptions. *commander-in-chief:* the Hebrew gives him his correct Assyrian title – *Tartan (turtanu)* as in 2 Kings 18: 17.

2. *sackcloth* appears to have been the recognized garment of a prophet (cp. Zech. 13: 4) apparently woven from some animal hair (Mark 1: 6 and cp. 2 Kings 1: 8). This is, however, the only reference to one of the 'writing' prophets wearing such a garment, and it may be that it was a characteristic of the prophetic guilds or cultic prophets, and deliberately adopted on this occasion by Isaiah as 'a badge of his profession', a further sign. Usually *sackcloth* is a sign of mourning (37: 1), and this may be the reason for this unusual attire. The

prophet first put on sackcloth as mourning for the death of
Ashdod. Then he walked about stripped of his outer garment
and barefoot as a captive going into exile.

3–4. The main purpose of this acted parable seems to be
directed against *Egypt*, and so by implication those who rely
on Egyptian help (verses 5–6). Ashdod was the first to be
conquered; Egypt was invaded in 671–667 B.C. In actual fact,
Egypt took little part in this revolt of 714–711, and when
Iamini, king of Ashdod, sought refuge in Egypt after the
collapse of the revolt, he was extradited to Assyria. ✳

FALLEN, FALLEN IS BABYLON

21   A wilderness: an oracle.

Rough weather, advancing like a storm in the south,
coming from the wilderness, from a land of terror!
2   Grim is the vision shown to me:
the traitor betrayed, the spoiler himself despoiled.
Up, Elam; up, Medes, to the siege,
   no time for weariness!
3   At this my limbs writhe in anguish,
I am gripped by pangs like a woman in labour.
I am distraught past hearing, dazed past seeing,
4   my mind reels, sudden convulsions seize me.

The cool twilight I longed for has become a terror:
5   the banquet is set out, the rugs are spread;
   they are eating and drinking –
rise, princes, burnish your shields.
6   For these were the words of the Lord to me:
Go, post a watchman to report what he sees.
7   He sees chariots, two-horsed chariots,
riders on asses, riders on camels.

He is alert, always on the alert.
> Then the look-out[a] cried: 8
All day long I stand on the Lord's watch-tower
and night after night I keep my station.
See, there come men in a chariot, a two-horsed chariot. 9
> And a voice calls back:
Fallen, fallen is Babylon,
and all the images of her gods lie shattered on the ground.
> O my people,   10
once trodden out and winnowed on the threshing-floor,
> what I have heard from the LORD of Hosts,
> from the God of Israel, I have told you.

✻ This passage, and also the two succeeding oracles, is difficult (a) to translate and (b) to interpret. The language is highly condensed and staccato in style, so that any readable English version must soften the effect. Most of the lines of the poem consist of only two Hebrew words! Add to this that the text has obviously suffered in the course of transmission and that the particular historical situation is by no means obvious. Even the title, 'A wilderness', is obscure. The one certain feature of the poem is that it relates to a disaster which has befallen, or is about to befall, Babylon (verse 9). That must be the starting-point in interpretation. An unexpected feature is the acute distress felt by the prophet at the disaster, though this finds a partial parallel in the fate of Moab (chs. 15–16).

Perhaps the most likely historical event to which this oracle refers is the collapse of the Babylonian power in 540 B.C. before the armies of Cyrus, king of Persia, after he had assumed the sovereignty by conquest over the Medes. Though this event brought relief and rejoicing to the prophet of chs. 13–14 and 40–55, the confusion and turmoil occasioned by the collapse

[a] *So Scroll; Heb.* a lion.

of an empire might also cause fear and apprehension. We should note, however, that Babylon also suffered defeat when on various occasions it rebelled against its Assyrian overlord in the eighth and seventh centuries. Both in 691 and 648 Babylon was savagely looted, while on the former occasion Sennacherib took away from Babylon the idol of its patron deity, Marduk (cp. verse 9). In the seventh century, the Elamites and Medes were also involved, but as allies of Babylon.

1. *wilderness:* the word is not more precisely defined, 'of the sea' in the Hebrew text being omitted in the N.E.B. with ancient versions. It is further defined by *in the south* (Hebrew *Negeb*) which often means the southern district of Judah, but also simply a compass point. If a sixth-century date is the background, the prophet is looking to the Arabian desert south of Babylon. If an earlier date is accepted, he is looking to the Judaean Negeb. *Rough weather...storm* would be the outward, natural event (cp. Ezek. 1: 4ff.) that stimulated the 'Grim...vision' of an invading army.

2. *betrayed...despoiled:* the English is ambiguous, being either past tenses active, or passive participles. The Hebrew gives active participles: 'the betrayer is betraying, the spoiler is spoiling'. The passive verbs require only a change of vowels in Hebrew. *no time for weariness* refers to the invaders, but the Hebrew 'all the sighing I have brought to an end' could refer to exiled peoples for whom such an invasion might bring release.

3. *past hearing...past seeing* or 'because of hearing – because of seeing', i.e. describing the prophetic experience of the word and the vision.

5. A vivid description of a *banquet* violently interrupted by a call to arms. The picture hardly suits Babylon in 538, for the city was surrendered without a fight. But it would be pedantic to take the vision too literally. It is possible that this passage prompted the account in Daniel 5.

6. A new word of the Lord to the prophet. Obviously the prophet cannot *post a watchman*; he does so in his visionary

experience, and then becomes himself the watchman (cp. Hab. 2: 1).

8. *look-out:* or alternatively 'he who sees' (that is, sees the vision), an older word for a prophet (1 Sam. 9: 9). *I* is very emphatic in the Hebrew sentence, indicating the prophet's loyal obedience.

9. In answer to the silent question 'What does this vision mean?' the divine message is given.

10. Restored to ordinary experience, the prophet tells those around him the vision and its meaning. To emphasize the certainty about what will happen, he uses the ancient titles of God, Israel's champion.　*

AN ORACLE FOR EDOM

Dumah: an oracle.　11

One calls to me from Seir:
Watchman, what is left of the night?
Watchman, what is left?
　The watchman answered:　12
Morning comes, and also night.[a]
Ask if you must; then come back again.

* This brief cryptic oracle is as obscure as *the night* of which it speaks. That it refers to Edom is clear from the reference to Seir. But *Dumah* is the name of an Arabian tribe or oasis (cp. Gen. 25: 14); the name in Hebrew as in English resembles Edom and the Septuagint so rendered it. But it may preserve a clue to the occasion of the oracle. Edom was, with other states, invaded by Arabian tribes in about 650 B.C., and many of its people fled to the southern part of Judah for refuge (cp. chs. 15–16). This would provide a suitable setting. Some Edomites sought an oracle from a Judaean prophet. 'How

[a] and also night: *or* and the night is full spent.

much longer are we to suffer this calamity?' The answer appears to mean 'A respite will come, but further calamity will follow' or it may mean 'Respite and calamity are both inevitable, determined by God.' He has no further word at present (cp. Jer. 42: 7) but invites the inquirers to come back again. ✷

AGAINST ARABIA

13 With the Arabs: an oracle.

You caravans of Dedan, that camp in the scrub with
    the Arabs,
14   bring water to meet the thirsty.
You dwellers in Tema, meet the fugitives with food,
15   for they flee from the sword, the sharp edge of the
    sword,
from the bent bow, and from the press of battle.

16 For these are the words of the Lord to me: Within a
year, as a hired labourer counts off the years, all the glory
17 of Kedar shall come to an end; few shall be the bows left
to the warriors of Kedar.
The LORD the God of Israel has spoken.

✷ The poetic oracle (13–15) is followed by a prose post-script (16–17). This historical situation may be that of Jer. 49: 28–33, which describes Nebuchadnezzar's attack, especially on Kedar.

13–14. The N.E.B. ignores the punctuation of the Hebrew Bible (Masoretic Text) in order to produce parallelism. If we retain the traditional punctuation, we should translate:

In the scrub with the Arabs you will camp, you caravans of
    Dedan,
To meet (the needs of) the thirsty, bring water;
You who dwell in the land of Tema,
Meet the fugitives with food.

The Dedanites were a South-Arabian tribe, east of the Red Sea. *Tema* was to the north of Dedan. If we follow the N.E.B. Dedan and Tema are to succour the fugitives (? from the Assyrian armies). If we follow the traditional punctuation, Tema is to give food and water to fugitives from Dedan.

16f. The doom of the Arabian tribe of *Kedar* is certain because Yahweh, God of Israel, has declared it. ✳

WITHOUT EXCUSE

The Valley of Vision:*ᵃ* an oracle.   **22**

Tell me, what is amiss
    that you have all climbed on to the roofs,
O city full of tumult, town in ferment   2
    and filled with uproar,
whose slain were not slain with the sword
    and did not die in battle?
        Your commanders are all in flight,   3
    huddled together out of bowshot;
all your stoutest warriors*ᵇ* are huddled together,
    they have taken to their heels.
Then I said, Turn your eyes away from me;   4
    leave me to weep in misery.
    Do not thrust consolation on me
    for the ruin of my own people.

For the Lord, the LORD of Hosts, has ordained a day   5
of tumult, a day of trampling and turmoil in the Valley
of Vision,*ᵃ* rousing cries for help that echo among the
mountains.

[a] *Or* of Calamity.
[b] your stoutest warriors; *so Sept.;* Heb. those found in you.

6   Elam took up his quiver,
  horses were harnessed to the chariots of Aram,[a]
  Kir took the cover from his shield.
7   Your fairest valleys were overrun by chariots and
    horsemen,
  the gates were hard beset,
8   the heart of Judah's defence was laid open.

On that day you looked to the weapons stored in the
9 House of the Forest; you filled all the many pools in the
City of David, collecting water from the Lower Pool.[b]
10 Then you surveyed the houses in Jerusalem, tearing some
11 down to make the wall inaccessible, and between the two
walls you made a cistern for the Waters of the Old Pool;
  but you did not look to the Maker of it all
  or consider him who fashioned it long ago.

12   On that day the Lord, the LORD of Hosts,
  called for weeping and beating the breast,
  for shaving the head and putting on sackcloth;
13   but instead there was joy and merry-making,
  slaughtering of cattle and killing of sheep,
  eating of meat and drinking of wine, as you thought,
  Let us eat and drink; for tomorrow we die.

14   The LORD of Hosts has revealed himself to me; in my
hearing he swore:

  Your wickedness shall never be purged
   until you die.
  This is the word of the Lord, the LORD of Hosts.

[a] *Prob. rdg.; Heb.* man.
[b] you filled…Lower Pool: *or* you took note of the cracks, many as
they were, in the wall of the City of David, and you collected water
from the Lower Pool.

* Although this passage is not specifically dated, the siege of Jerusalem and the lifting of the siege after Hezekiah's submission in 701 B.C. would provide the most likely setting (cp. Isa. 36–9). An earlier date in 711 B.C. when Jerusalem seemed to be threatened but escaped the fate of Ashdod (ch. 20) has been suggested, but there is no suggestion that on that occasion Hezekiah's army was involved (cp. verses 3–4) or that Judah was invaded (verses 7–8). Both from the Old Testament and from Sennacherib's annals we know that in the rebellion of 703–701, the land was invaded, its principal towns devastated, and Hezekiah was 'shut up like a bird in a cage'. The situation was so desperate that some of Hezekiah's troops deserted and were captured (2b–3); many more had died of disease and starvation in the besieged city. It is true that the siege was lifted after the imposition of heavy tribute, but joy and merry-making was totally out of place. But the gravity of Isaiah's judgement goes deeper. Hezekiah had made all military preparations, gathered weapons, strengthened the defences, provided a water-supply, but had given no thought to the judgement of God about which Isaiah had given clear warning. The lifting of the siege of Jerusalem may well have been unsuspected and better than its inhabitants could have hoped for, but it should have been an occasion for penitence and a serious attempt to seek God's will. Judgement was postponed, not annulled.

1. *Vision:* here and in verse 5 the Hebrew *ḥizzayon* may be a deliberate distortion of *ḥinnom*, a place where human sacrifice was offered to a pagan deity (2 Kings 23: 10), Gehenna of the New Testament.

2. *uproar* is the noisy jubilation over the departure of the Assyrian army.

3. *stoutest warriors:* the N.E.B. requires a slight emendation supported by the Septuagint.

4. The prophet alone grieves over the dead and the general devastation of Judah, the greater part of which was taken from Hezekiah and given to the Philistines, who had remained loyal to Assyria.

5. Isaiah can hear, above the noise of the exultant throng, the *cries for help* from fugitives in Judah's hill-country. This had happened through the mistaken policy of the government which ignored God's judgement.

6-7. Refers to various elements in the Assyrian army. *Aram* for the Hebrew *adam*.

8. *House of the Forest* so called because of the cedar pillars that supported the roof. It was built by Solomon as an armoury (2 Kings 7: 2; 10: 17).

9. The reference is to the digging of the Siloam tunnel which brought water into the city (2 Kings 20:20). An inscription on the walls of this tunnel records the satisfaction felt at the success of this engineering feat. The labourers had started from both ends and met in the middle 'pick against pick'.

11. The judgement at the end of the verse resembles that levelled against Sennacherib in 37: 26. Hezekiah and Sennacherib are alike confronted by the sovereign lord of history whom they ignore.

12-13. God appointed this day as a day of national repentance. Jerusalem has turned it into hysterical feasting. 'Why not? Tomorrow we may all be killed!' As Isaiah saw it, this was the inevitable outcome of politics that ignored God.

14. Death is inevitable indeed for those who have rejected the living God. ✳

SHEBNA AND ELIAKIM

15 These were the words of the Lord, the LORD of Hosts:

Go to this steward,
to Shebna, comptroller of the household, and say:
16 What right, what business, have you here,
that you have dug yourself a grave here,
cutting out your grave on a height
and carving yourself a resting-place in the rock?

The LORD will shake you out,   17
  shake you as a garment[a] is shaken out
  to rid it of lice;
then he will bundle you tightly and throw you   18
like a ball into a great wide land.
  There you shall die,
  and there shall lie your chariot of honour,
  an object of contempt to your master's household.
I will remove you from office and drive[b] you from your 19
  post.

On that day I will send for my servant Eliakim son of   20
Hilkiah; I will invest him with your robe, gird him with   21
your sash; and hand over your authority to him. He shall
be a father to the inhabitants of Jerusalem and the people
of Judah. I will lay the key of the house of David on his 22
shoulder; what he opens no man shall shut, and what he
shuts no man shall open. He shall be a seat of honour for 23
his father's family; I will fasten him firmly in place like
a peg. On him shall hang all the weight of the family,   24
down to the lowest dregs[c] – all the little vessels, both bowls
and pots. On that day, says the LORD of Hosts, the peg   25
which was firmly fastened in its place shall be removed;
it shall be hacked out and shall fall, and the load of things
hanging on it shall be destroyed. The LORD has spoken.

* It is not usual for the Old Testament prophets to utter an
oracle against individuals other than kings. The particular
instances show these individuals as opposing the prophet in
his divinely commissioned work (Amos 7: 16f.; Jer. 20: 1–6;
28: 12–17; cp. 1 Kings 22: 25). The grounds for the indictment

[a] *Prob. rdg.; Heb.* man.   [b] *So Pesh.; Heb.* he will drive.
[c] down to the lowest dregs: *lit.* dung and excrement.

of Shebna are not given; his building of a rock-tomb is hardly adequate as a reason. It is possible that, as a member of the royal council, he had taken the lead in advising Hezekiah to rebel against Assyria and to seek help from Egypt.

15. *steward:* the word, although known outside the Old Testament, is not otherwise used for a court official. (The feminine form is used in 1 Kings 1: 2, 4.) It is possible that the word is not the name for an office; the term for *comptroller of the household* is a regular title. The phrase *this steward* suggests a note of derision conveyed by the voice more easily than in writing. We might almost say 'this lackey'. It has been suggested that he was in the pay of a foreign power, e.g. Egypt. He was removed from his office as comptroller, but made 'adjutant general' (36: 3, where the Hebrew word means 'secretary' but, like the English 'Secretary of State', acquired a further significance by usage). The same Hebrew word is used at 2 Kings 12: 10 (N.E.B. 'secretary'). Evidently, even though he was dismissed from his original office, he was not in disgrace. A tomb has been discovered on a hillside opposite Jerusalem with an inscription bearing a name (partly defaced) of a *comptroller* belonging to this period. The name has, with some hesitation, been identified with that of Shebna. Whether he was buried there is not known.

16. Shebna was preparing a rock-tomb appropriate to his high office.

17. The prophet declared that he will die in disgrace or in exile. *garment* (see footnote *a*) is an emendation of the Hebrew for '(strong) man'. If the Hebrew is retained, it is a scornful term: 'The LORD will fling you away, Big Man...'.

20–3. The high praise given to *Eliakim* in these verses is in strong contrast to verse 25. It has been suggested that the doom on Eliakim is due to a later disciple who knew of Eliakim's disgrace. In that case verse 24 gives the reason; he has used his high position to favour members of his own family.

22. *the key of the house of David:* a symbol of full authority delegated by the king (cp. Matt. 16: 19; Rev. 3: 7). The *key*

in Palestine was an object of considerable size and was proudly carried in public on state occasions.

23. *peg:* i.e. a tent peg, but in verse 24 a large peg fixed into the wall of a house. ✻

ORACLES AGAINST TYRE

Tyre: an oracle.   **23**

The ships of Tarshish howl, for the harbour is sacked;
the port of entry from Kittim is swept away.
   The people of the sea-coast, the merchants of Sidon, 2–3
      wail,
  people whose agents*a* cross the great waters,
    whose harvest*b* is the grain of the Shihor
    and their revenue the trade of nations.
Sidon, the sea-fortress,*c* cries in her disappointment,*d* 4
I no longer feel the anguish of labour or bear children;
I have no young sons to rear, no daughters to bring up.
   When the news is confirmed in Egypt   5
   her people sway in anguish at the fate of Tyre.
    Make your way to Tarshish, they say,   6
    howl, you who dwell by the sea-coast.
  Is this your busy city, ancient in story,   7
on whose voyages you were carried to settle far away?

Whose plan was this against Tyre, the city of battle-   8
     ments,
   whose merchants were princes
   and her traders the most honoured men on earth?

[a] whose agents: *prob. rdg., cp. Scroll; Heb.* they have filled you.
[b] whose harvest: *prob. rdg.; Heb.* the harvest of the Nile.
[c] the sea-fortress: *prob. rdg.; Heb.* the sea, sea-fortress, saying.
[d] in her disappointment: *prob. rdg.; Heb.* be disappointed.

9 The LORD of Hosts planned it to prick every noble's pride
and bring all the most honoured men on earth into
contempt.

10 Take to the tillage of your fields,[a] you people of
Tarshish;
for your market[b] is lost.

11 The LORD has stretched out his hand over the sea
and shaken kingdoms,
he has given his command to destroy the marts of
Canaan;

12 and he has said, You shall busy yourselves no more,
you, the sorely oppressed virgin city of Sidon.
Though you arise and cross over to Kittim,
even there you shall find no rest.

13 Look at this land, the destined home of ships[c]! The
Chaldaeans[d] erected their[e] siege-towers, dismantled its
palaces and laid it in ruins.

14 Howl, you ships of Tarshish;
for your haven is sacked.

15 From that day Tyre shall be forgotten for seventy years,
the span of one king's life. At the end of the seventy years
her plight shall be that of the harlot in the song:

16 Take your harp, go round the city,
poor forgotten harlot;
touch the strings sweetly, sing all your songs,
make men remember you again.

17 At the end of seventy years, the LORD will turn again to

[a] Take...fields: *so Sept.; Heb.* Pass over your fields like the Nile.
[b] *Prob. rdg.; Heb.* girdle.   [c] *Or* marmots.
[d] *Prob. rdg.; Heb. adds* this was the people; it was not Assyria.
[e] *Prob. rdg.; Heb.* his.

Tyre; she shall go back to her old trade and hire herself out to every kingdom on earth. The profits of her trading 18 will be dedicated to the LORD; they shall not be hoarded or stored up, but shall be given to those who worship[a] the LORD, to purchase food in plenty and fine attire.

* The main theme of this chapter is clear. The great maritime empire of Phoenicia will collapse. The occasion for this is pride, the downfall is ordained by God. Finally a new generation, in its humiliation purged of its pride, will restore Phoenicia's prosperity, but now to sustain the people of God.

In detail the difficulties are considerable. As the footnotes show, the text has suffered in the course of transmission. Some conjectural emendation is inevitable. No less difficult is it to date the various parts of the chapter, or to determine the exact extent of each oracle. It is possible that Isaiah was the speaker of verses 1–7 and 8–12, but if so his expectations were far from realized as verses 13f. make clear. Verses 15f. and 17f. are evidently later additions; the latter certainly refers to no known historical situation.

The Phoenicians were an important maritime nation in the ancient world, their principal cities being Tyre, Sidon, Byblos and Ugarit (Ras Shamra). The name is the Greek equivalent of Canaan, itself derived from a word meaning purple dye obtained from a shellfish. In the course of their trading, they established colonies on the North African coast, such as Carthage, on Sardinia and in Spain. Their trading relationships with Solomon are referred to in 1 Kings 5. Their period of commercial and colonial expansion was greatest from about 1000 to 700 B.C. Thereafter they suffered from Assyrian attacks and the growing rivalry of the Greeks. It was the Phoenicians who transmitted to the Greeks the system of alphabetic writing from which ultimately our own system derives. Phoenicia was first attacked by Assyria in 701 B.C.

[a] *Lit.* sit in the presence of.

and on various occasions in the following century, but not destroyed. During Sennacherib's attack, the king of Tyre fled to Cyprus, and this may be referred to in verse 12. Tyre was besieged by Nebuchadnezzar in 585 until 573: he was unable to reduce it (cp. Ezek. 29: 17ff.) but its old importance was destroyed and it became a vassal state of the Babylonian empire. In 333 B.C., in spite of its resistance, it was reduced by Alexander the Great.

This brief sketch will indicate both the tone of these oracles and the difficulty of dating them. They should be read alongside Ezek. 26–8. Following the N.E.B. we may recognize two oracles, 1–7 and 8–12, where the two cities Sidon and Tyre signify Phoenicia as a whole; and three subsequent additions 13f., 15f., 17f., the last two being post-exilic.

1. *Tyre* in the title would be natural to a Judaean since this was the Phoenician city with which Jerusalem had most contact. *ships of Tarshish:* originally ships carrying cargo from copper refineries in Sardinia and Spain. The word *tarshish* means refinery and Tartessus in Spain was derived from it (cp. 2: 16). *Kittim* is Cyprus. The second line could also be rendered: 'Coming from the land of Cyprus, it was revealed to them', i.e. the sailors learned of the fate of Sidon as they returned from Cyprus.

2–3. *the Shihor:* 'the waters of Horus', i.e. the Nile.

4. A vivid description of the destruction of *Sidon*, after which the merchants no longer sail the Mediterranean.

7. A reference to Phoenician colonies in the western Mediterranean, e.g. Carthage and Tartessus.

10. With the loss of her maritime trade the people of Tartessus are reduced to an agricultural economy.

11. *Canaan:* the Assyrian name for Phoenicia.

12. *busy yourselves:* or exult.

13. The Hebrew text (see footnote *d*) makes it clear that this was a later addition. The defeat of the Phoenicians expected by the prophet was not fully realized. It was to be accomplished by the Babylonian army (*the Chaldeans*).

14. The introductory oracle (verse 1) is repeated.

15f. Apparently an addition referring to the destruction by Alexander. *seventy years* is a conventional figure (cp. Jer. 25: 11–12). The *song* of the *harlot* refers to Tyrian trade, plying her wares far and wide. Compare Rev. 18: 3.

17f. This is apparently based on 60: 4–14, and expresses an aspect of the Jewish expectation of the Golden Age. *turn again* is hardly adequate to the Hebrew verb, which in Jer. 29: 10 is rendered by 'I will take up your cause' or in Ps. 8: 4 'care for'. Especially in the light of the Jeremiah passage, some such meaning must be intended here. ✶

The LORD's judgement on
the earth

✶ Chapters 24–7 of the book of Isaiah are often called the Isaiah Apocalypse. This is a misleading description since its form is not like that of Daniel or The Revelation of John, and still less like the apocalyptic writings, Jewish and Christian, of the first centuries B.C. and A.D. What they have in common is a preoccupation with the final victory of God over evil and therefore a universal judgement, the great banquet associated with the celebration of the Lord's enthronement, the destruction of the ever-threatening chaos monster, and the final salvation of the loyal people of God. But these chapters lack the characteristics of the apocalyptists such as visions needing angelic interpretations, the re-interpretations of scriptures to new situations of crisis, the identification of pagan nations with mythical beasts, such mysterious numbers as we find in Dan. 7: 25; 8: 14, and the tendency towards Dualism, that is, the idea of a conflict between God and the spirit or spirits of evil – although in Jewish thought God's final victory was

143

always assured. It is reasonable to suggest that the contents of these chapters, together with some other parts of the Old Testament (e.g. Ezek. 38-9; Joel; and Zech. 9-14) provided the material out of which apocalyptic writing developed. But this is a distinctive form of prophecy, probably the final expression of the Isaianic school of disciples. Beyond saying that it is post-exilic, it would be hazardous to define the date; probably some time in the fourth century B.C. would provide the appropriate setting. Earlier attempts to associate these chapters with the Maccabaean era are most unlikely in view of the fact that they form part of the Isaiah scroll as used by the Dead Sea covenanters (see *The Making of the Old Testament*, pp. 101-4). These chapters seem to indicate a world in confusion, in the political upheavals of which the Jews were inevitably involved, yet in no way responsible. It was in the fourth century that the struggle for supremacy between Persia and Greece was taking place, a struggle in which the political stability of the world was threatened. In many respects the conditions of the post-war world of our time would form a fitting context for these chapters. Where in the midst of confusion is there any ground for hope? What contribution has religion to offer? Clearly the old nature-religions are ill equipped to meet these strains, and religion deriving from national supremacy can hardly survive. It may be regarded as one of the triumphs of Israel's faith, mediated through prophet and cultus, that in these chapters it could not only survive but prove victorious.

These chapters contain prophecies of the end of the age interspersed with psalms and prayers. So skilfully have they been woven together that it is not always obvious where prophecy ends and psalm begins. This would suggest that whatever be the origin of the various elements, they have been brought together by one writer. He may well be the prophet-disciple in the Isaiah tradition seeking to re-interpret the master's mind in a situation which in many ways differed greatly from those of the eighth century. While as a whole the contents of these chapters differ considerably from the oracles of Isaiah in style, vocabulary, ideas and experience and the circumstances which are assumed, there are also similarities. This may suggest that the prophecies were first uttered among the continuing society of Isaiah's disciples whose faith was threatened by the apparent collapse of God's world-order; that when they had proved effective within that circle, they were included within the final collection of Isaiah's oracles for wider publication among the Jewish community. If this is a right understanding of these chapters, they are a fine exposition of the faith: God is the same, yesterday, today and for ever.

This weaving together of prophecy and psalm into an overall unity has suggested the description of the contents as prophetic liturgy or liturgies used by a community as they faced a world in turmoil and confusion. Prophecy merges into, and apparently modifies, remembered psalms, each combining with the other to strengthen the faith and hope of the believers. The theme is that the confusion in the world has been brought about by man's sin, but in fact it is God's judgement, in which he is also working for the salvation of the faithful. The new age of peace and security is about to dawn. Death itself will be done away and the dead shall be raised to share in the new creation. The movement of thought seems to have been influenced by the Flood story of Gen. 6-9; cp. 24: 5, 20; 26: 20. We may make the following divisions of the contents: 24: 1-20; 24: 21 – 25: 12; 26: 1-19; 26: 20 – 27: 13.

Within these are the main divisions, which have sometimes been called prophetic liturgies; the limits of the various elements that have gone to make up the whole are not so easily determined. The following may be suggested as a possible division: Prophecy, 24: 1-3, 17-20, 21-3; 25: 6-8; 26: 20-1; 27: 1, 12-13. Poems of various kinds, 24: 4-6, 7-9, 10-13 are laments; 24: 14-16 a hymn that ends with the poet's cry of distress; 25: 1-5, 9-12; 26: 1-6 are hymns; 26: 7-19

prayers (to which 26: 20–1 is the divine answer); 27: 2–6 is
God's song, possibly uttered by a prophet in the worshipping
congregation; 27: 7–11 a reflective poem. ✻

UNIVERSAL JUDGEMENT

24 Beware, the LORD will empty the earth,
　　　split it open and turn it upside down,
　　　　　and scatter its inhabitants.

2　　　Then it will be the same for priest and people,
　　　the same for master and slave, mistress and slave-girl,
　　　　　seller and buyer,
　　　borrower and lender, debtor and creditor.

3　　　The earth is emptied clean away
　　　　　and stripped clean bare.
　　　For this is the word that the LORD has spoken.

4　　　The earth dries up and withers,
　　　　the whole world withers and grows sick;
　　　　　the earth's high places[a] sicken,

5　　　and earth itself is desecrated by the feet of those who
　　　　　live in it,
　　　because they have broken the laws, disobeyed the
　　　　　statutes
　　　　and violated the eternal covenant.

6　　For this a curse has devoured the earth
　　　　and its inhabitants stand aghast.
　　　For this those who inhabit the earth dwindle
　　　　and only a few men are left.

7　　　The new wine dries up, the vines sicken,
　　　　and all the revellers turn to sorrow.

[a] the earth's high places: *so Sept.; Heb.* the height of the people of
earth.

Silent the merry beat of tambourines,   8
hushed the shouts of revelry,
the merry harp is silent.
No one shall drink wine to the sound of song;   9
the liquor will be bitter to the man who drinks it.
The city of chaos is a broken city,   10
every house barred, that no one may enter.
Men call for wine in the streets;   11
all revelry is darkened,
and mirth is banished from the land.

Desolation alone is left in the city   12
and the gate is broken into pieces.
So shall it be in all the world, in every nation,   13
as when an olive-tree is beaten and stripped,
as when the vintage is ended.

Men raise their voices and cry aloud,   14
they shout in the west,[a] so great is the LORD's majesty.
Therefore let the LORD be glorified in the regions of   15
the east,[b]
and the name of the LORD the God of Israel
in the coasts and islands of the west.

From the ends of the earth we have heard them sing,   16
How lovely is righteousness!
But I thought, Villainy, villainy!
Woe to the traitors[c] and their treachery!
Traitors double-dyed they are indeed!
The hunter's scare, the pit, and the trap   17
threaten all who dwell in the land;

[a] in the west: *or* more loudly than the sea.
[b] the regions of the east: *mng. of Heb. word uncertain.*
[c] *So Sept.; Heb.* Woe to me, traitors.

18   if a man runs from the rattle of the scare
        he will fall into the pit;
    if he climbs out of the pit
        he will be caught in the trap.
    When the windows of heaven above are opened
        and earth's foundations shake,
19   the earth is utterly shattered.
    it is convulsed and reels wildly.
20   The earth reels to and fro like a drunken man
        and sways like a watchman's shelter;
    the sins of men weigh heavy upon it,
    and it falls to rise no more.

✴ Verses 1–3, 13 is an oracle into which the laments have been inserted. The judgement is imminent; it will be as sudden and as devastating as an earthquake and the whole social order will be disrupted. There are echoes here of Hos. 4, but now extended to affect the whole world. The paired words *priest...people* is appropriate to the post-exilic situation where high priest was the political as well as the ecclesiastical head of the community.

4–6. A lament over the land suffering from prolonged drought is extended to the whole *earth*.

5. This gives the reason in words reminiscent of the Flood story, but more serious since the *eternal covenant* of Gen. 9: 11–17 has been broken. This can only mean a return to chaos.

7–13. This is based on a vintage song, but the joy appropriate to vintage has become a lament for the vintage that has failed. *city of chaos* need not refer to a particular city but could be a general term. The life of a city depends on the acceptance by its inhabitants of an orderly way of life. When law and order are disregarded, chaos ensues; civilization has broken down.

14–16. By contrast with the hymn of praise normally sung to celebrate God's rule (cp. Pss. 96, 97) the prophet must warn of the imminence of devastating judgement because of wide-spread treachery.

17–20. This continues the prophecy of verse 13 and is reminiscent of Jer. 48: 43f.; cp. also Amos 5: 19. *windows of heaven* (cp. Gen. 7: 11); similar language is used in the Ras Shamra tablets. The ancient world thought of the sky as a separating wall holding back the water, which was allowed to come through vents as rain.

20. *it falls*... a quotation from Amos 5: 2, but applied here to the whole earth. ✻

THE RULE OF GOD AND HIS ROYAL BANQUET

On that day the LORD will punish   21
the host of heaven in heaven, and on earth the kings of
    the earth,
herded together, close packed like prisoners in a   22
    dungeon;
shut up in gaol, after a long time they shall be punished.
The moon shall grow pale and the sun hide its face in 23
    shame;
    for the LORD of Hosts has become king
    on Mount Zion and in Jerusalem,
    and shows his glory before their elders.

The deliverance and ingathering of Judah

O LORD, thou art my God;   **25**
I will exalt thee and praise thy name;
    for thou hast accomplished a wonderful purpose,

certain and sure, from of old.

2   For thou hast turned cities[a] into heaps of ruin,
and fortified towns into rubble;
every mansion in the cities is swept away,
    never to be rebuilt.

3   For this a cruel nation holds thee in honour,
the cities of ruthless nations fear thee.

4   Truly thou hast been a refuge to the poor,
a refuge to the needy in his trouble,
shelter from the tempest and shade from the heat.
For the blast of the ruthless is like an icy storm

5   or a scorching drought;
    thou subduest the roar of the foe,[b]
and the song of the ruthless dies away.

6   On this mountain the LORD of Hosts will prepare
    a banquet of rich fare for all the peoples,
a banquet of wines well matured and richest fare,
    well-matured wines strained clear.

7   On this mountain the LORD will swallow up
that veil that shrouds all the peoples,
the pall thrown over all the nations;

8   he will swallow up death for ever.
Then the Lord GOD will wipe away the tears
    from every face
and remove the reproach of his people from the whole
    earth.
The LORD has spoken.

9   On that day men will say,
See, this is our God

[a] cities: *so Sept.; Heb.* from a city.
[b] *Prob. rdg.; Heb. adds* heat in the shadow of a cloud.

for whom we have waited to deliver us;
this is the LORD for whom we have waited;
let us rejoice and exult in his deliverance.
For the hand of the LORD will rest on this mountain,   10
but Moab shall be trampled under his feet
as straw is trampled into a midden.
In it Moab shall spread out his hands   11
as a swimmer spreads his hands to swim,
but he shall sink his pride with every stroke of his hands.
The LORD has thrown down the high defences of   12
your walls,
has levelled them to the earth
and brought them down to the dust.

* 21–3. The rule of God is depicted after the manner of an
earthly king's enthronement (cp. Ps. 93) which recent studies
have suggested was annually celebrated in the temple. But,
while that was usually associated with the praise for his effective maintenance of the good order of the world which he had
created, here it is associated with his punishment of his enemies
celestial and terrestrial. This theme is taken up later in apocalyptic literature. The closing line of verse 23 refers to Exod.
24: 9f. when the seventy elders beheld the glory of God. The
covenant comes to its fulfilment.

25: 1–5. A hymn celebrating God's active rule, his victory
over all oppression and the release of the oppressed people
of God. It appears to be a much older hymn celebrating the
overthrow of a *cruel nation*, possibly Babylon or Nineveh,
but used in this new context (cp. Isa. 13). The language of
verse 1 appears to be a deliberate allusion to Exod. 15: 2, 11
as though to say 'As God by his wonderful work rescued his
people from Egypt, so now even more wonderfully he is
about to fulfil his redemptive purpose.' *

6–8. The coronation banquet. This passage follows on 24:

151

21–3. Just as the earthly king at his enthronement held a coronation feast (cp. 1 Kings 1: 9, 25) so the divine king is depicted. The same theme is found in Canaanite mythology and evidently formed part of the mental furniture of the people of Palestine. The very phrase in verse 8 'he will swallow up death' is a subtle use of popular language, for in the Canaanite myth Baal destroys Môt (= Hebrew *maweth*, death). This theme of the great banquet continues into later apocalyptic literature, cp. Rev. 19: 17. But the biblical writers turn this popular thought to their own purpose. This triumph of God marks the end of history with its mysterious tale of sorrow and suffering, and death, the last enemy, is itself destroyed. What in the Canaanite myth was a dramatic portrayal of the annual death and revival of vegetation, was transformed into a once-and-for-all event, the fulfilment of God's majestic purpose for his people. This is what is presented with a new certainty in Rev. 21: 4. It seems probable that this forms part of the thinking in the presentation of the Lord's Supper in the New Testament, especially 1 Cor. 15: 22–7.

6. *On this mountain* refers back to 24: 23, 'Zion'. The *rich fare* and *wines* are more than food; they are symbols of life.

7. The *veil* and *pall* are symbols of mourning for the dead. The joy of the banquet is not for the Jew only, but for all mankind.

9–12. This contains a hymn of praise whose original conclusion was probably at 10*a* – man's response of joy at the announcement of God's final triumph. What follows (10*b*–12) appears to be an older doom oracle on *Moab*, such as we find in Isa. 15–16; Jer. 48, added here to typify all that is hostile to God's purpose. The vivid but ugly portrayal of the enemy as a man vainly struggling to escape from a dung-pit (*midden*) is, to our ears, hardly in keeping with the tone of what precedes. ✷

A HYMN AND PRAYERS OF LAMENT

On that day this song shall be sung in Judah: **26**

We have a strong city
whose walls and ramparts are our deliverance.
Open the gates to let a righteous nation in,   2
a nation that keeps faith.
Thou dost keep in peace men of constant mind,   3
in peace because they trust in thee.
Trust in the LORD for ever;   4
for the LORD himself is an everlasting rock.
He has brought low all who dwell high in a towering   5
city;
he levels it[a] to the ground and lays it in the dust,
that the oppressed and the poor may tread it underfoot.   6
The path of the righteous is level,   7
and thou markest out the right way for the upright.
We too look to[b] the path prescribed in thy laws, O LORD;   8
thy name and thy memory are our heart's desire.
With all my heart I long for thee in the night,   9
I seek thee eagerly when dawn breaks;
for, when thy laws prevail in the land,
the inhabitants of the world learn justice.
The wicked are destroyed, they have never learnt justice;   10
corrupt in a land of honest ways,
they do not regard the majesty of the LORD.

O LORD, thy hand is lifted high,   11
but the bitter enemies of thy[c] people do not see it;[d]

[a] *So Scroll; Heb. repeats* he levels it. [b] *So Scroll; Heb.* We look to thee. [c] thy: *prob. rdg., cp. Targ.; Heb. om.* [d] *Prob. rdg.; Heb. adds* let them see and be ashamed.

let the fire of thy enmity destroy them.

12 O LORD, thou wilt bestow prosperity on us;
for in truth all our works are thy doing.

13 O LORD our God,
other lords than thou have been our masters,
but thee alone do we invoke by name.

14 The dead will not live again,
those long in their graves will not rise;
to this end thou hast punished them and destroyed
them,
and made all memory of them perish.

15 Thou hast enlarged the nation, O LORD,
enlarged it and won thyself honour,
thou hast extended all the frontiers of the land.

16 In our distress, O LORD, we*a* sought thee out,
chastened by the mere whisper of thy rebuke.

17 As a woman with child, when her time is near,
is in labour and cries out in her pains,
so were we in thy presence, O LORD.

18 We have been with child, we have been in labour,*b*
but have brought forth wind.
We have won no success for the land,
and no one will be born to inhabit the world.

19 But thy dead live, their bodies*c* will rise again.
They that sleep in the earth will awake and shout for
joy;
for thy dew is a dew of sparkling light,
and the earth will bring those long dead to birth
again.

[a] *Prob. rdg.; Heb.* they.   [b] *Prob. rdg., cp. Sept.; Heb. adds* like.
[c] *So Pesh.; Heb.* my body.

Go, my people, enter your rooms   20
    and shut your doors behind you;
withdraw for a brief while, until wrath has gone by.
For see, the LORD is coming from his place   21
to punish the inhabitants of the earth for their sins;
    then the earth shall uncover her blood-stains
    and hide her slain no more.

✳ 1–6. Praise for the final victory. This may be an older
liturgy for a ceremonial procession to celebrate a victory
(cp. Pss. 24: 7–10; 118: 19–20). Used in this context it cele-
brates God's final triumph. The *strong city* refers to Jerusalem.
A more literal translation of the Hebrew would mean that
God makes his victorious *deliverance* the *walls and ramparts*. History had shown that the physical walls were no
protection.

2. *Open* is a plural imperative addressed to those inside the
temple.

4. *everlasting rock* recalls an ancient title for God (cp. Pss.
18: 2; 95: 1) pointing to him as protector.

5. *towering city:* this may originally have meant a particular
city, but is here a general term for the proud and arrogant;
cp. Obad. verses 3–4.

7–10. A prayer. It opens with a wisdom saying, verse 7,
which forms the theme of the prayer that follows. The change
from plural (verse 8) to singular (verse 9) is common in such
entreaties. The prayer of the community becomes focused in
the heart of the leader.

8. *name:* this is more than a label; it is an essential part of
the person. *memory:* i.e., the opening of the mind to receive
all the saving work of God which he did in the exodus.
Thus the verse indicates the whole-hearted desire for that
intimate relationship with God the Saviour that he offers in
the covenant.

11–18. The lament of the congregation. The prayer is

almost a conversation with God in which present oppression is set against the background of divine promise of prosperity.

14. *The dead* are the oppressive heathen rulers, who have usurped God's authority in the land.

15. This verse recalls the glorious kingdom of David.

16–18. These verses recall the present weakness and distress. The situation is apparently hopeless.

19. This must be the divine answer through his prophet as he prays, picking up the very words of verse 14, reversing them and applying them to the sorrowing people of God. It is one of the most remarkable reversals in the Bible, the more so in that there was nothing which could prepare the mind for this affirmation. Israel's thought had not extended to life after death, as we see from Pss. 88: 5, 10–12; 115: 17; Job 10: 21f. Partly this may have been due to its revulsion from necromancy and various forms of spiritism; partly too to its emphasis on Yahweh as the living God so that the shadowy realm of the dead would be outside his jurisdiction. Yet there were some preparations, chiefly in the form of a national resurrection, as in Ezek. 37: 1–14. Thus the verse, like that of Dan. 12: 2, looks not for mere survival, nor does it rest on a belief in the immortality of some element (soul or spirit) of human personality. It looks for a divine act of resurrection, so that the depopulated land will be filled again with the people of God. We may see here the beginning of that confident hope that was to reach maturity in the Christian doctrine.

20–1. The prophet speaks. In the light of his new faith, a great deliverance is at hand. The faithful community can, like Noah of old (Gen. 7: 16) or like the slaves in Egypt (Exod. 12: 22–3) await with confidence the day of judgement on God's opponents. The guilt of the murderers will be no longer unrequited. ✣

TRIUMPH OVER CHAOS

On that day the LORD will punish   **27**
with his cruel sword, his mighty and powerful sword,
    Leviathan that twisting[a] sea-serpent,
    that writhing serpent Leviathan,
    and slay the monster of the deep.

✻ The oracle is cast in the form of an ancient Canaanite myth
to which there are several allusions in the Old Testament (cp.
Ps. 74: 12–14). Just as in the ancient myth the god had
destroyed the chaos monster in order to establish the ordered
world of nature, so will Yahweh God of Israel crush all disorder in the life of mankind and bring about the good order
of the Kingdom of God. ✻

A NEW SONG OF THE VINEYARD

On that day sing to the pleasant[b] vineyard,   2
    I the LORD am its keeper,   3
moment by moment I water it for fear its green leaves
    fail.
    Night and day I tend it,
        but I get no wine;   4
    I would as soon have briars and thorns,
then I would wage war upon it and burn it all up,
unless it grasps me as its refuge and makes peace with
    me –
    unless it makes peace with me.   5

In time to come Jacob's offspring shall take root   6
and Israel shall bud and blossom,
    and they shall fill the whole earth with fruit.

    [a] *Or* primeval.   [b] *So Sept.; Heb.* wine.

✻ The vineyard song of Isaiah 5: 1–7 with its word of condemnation is recast to become a song of hope in the protective care of God. True the vineyard, Israel, had been unproductive so that the vine seemed no better than (gentile) briars, but being reconciled to God, it will bear much fruit for the benefit of all mankind. ✻

REFLECTION ON ISRAEL'S HISTORY

7 Has God struck him down as he struck others down?
 Has the slayer been slain as he slew others?
8–10[a] This then purges Jacob's iniquity,
  this[b] has removed his sin:
 that he grinds all altar stones to powder like chalk;
  no sacred poles and incense-altars are left standing.

 The fortified city is left solitary,
  and his quarrel with her ends in brushing her away,[c]
 removing her by a cruel blast when the east wind
   blows;
 it is a homestead stripped bare, deserted like a wilderness;
  there the calf grazes and there lies down,
   and crops every twig.
11 Its boughs snap off when they grow dry,
 and women come and light their fires with them.
  For they are a people without sense;
  therefore their maker will show them no mercy,
   he who formed them will show them no favour.

[a] *Verses 8–10 re-arranged thus: 9, 10a, 8, 10b.*
[b] *Prob. rdg.; Heb. adds* all fruit.
[c] *Prob. rdg.; Heb. adds* by dismissing her.

* These verses are not obviously related to what precedes or follows. They may be divided into two parts as in the N.E.B. The first poem, if the N.E.B. division of the verses (see foot-note) is correct, appears to refer to an invasion in which Israel has suffered the same fate as other nations, so that apparently God has not protected his people. But if Israel will destroy all signs of idolatrous worship, this will expiate the *iniquity*. It may well be a much older poem, perhaps from the time of the Babylonian or even Assyrian invasion.

The same date would be appropriate for the second poem, suggesting the conditions after the invasion has ended, leaving a devastated land. There are echoes in verse 11 in the Hebrew, of Isa. 1: 3 (*without sense*) and Hos. 1: 6 (*no mercy*). *

TWO ORACLES OF RESTORATION

On that day the LORD will beat out the grain,   12
from the streams of the Euphrates to the Torrent of
    Egypt;
but you Israelites will be gleaned
   one by one.

On that day   13
a blast shall be blown on a great trumpet,
   and those who are lost in Assyria
and those dispersed in Egypt will come in
and worship the LORD on the holy mountain, in
    Jerusalem.

* The first oracle (12) speaks of the day of the Lord under the figure of a great harvest which will restore the land referred to by its ideal boundaries as promised to Abraham (Gen. 15: 18) and realized under David and Solomon (1 Kings 4: 21). The Jewish community will be carefully separated from the Gentiles. *gleaned* indicates the care with which God

will treat each one of his people as he separates them from the chaff.

The second oracle, under a quite different figure, brings these four chapters to their true conclusion. The *great trumpet*, more accurately 'the ram's horn', originally used to summon to the holy war was later used to summon the people of God to celebrate and 'hallow the fiftieth year and proclaim liberation' (Lev. 25: 10). Thus all Israel, dispersed as they are throughout the world, will be gathered to a supreme act of worship. A similar emphasis on worship as the climax of God's work of salvation appears in Joel 2: 15f. and in Rev. 19. ✱

Assyria and Judah

✱ This section (chs. 28–33) of the book of Isaiah returns to the eighth century B.C., mainly, apart from the opening oracle, from the closing years of that century with occasional comments from a later period. ✱

BEFUDDLED LEADERS

28   Oh, the proud garlands of the drunkards of Ephraim
          and the flowering sprays, so lovely in their beauty,
    on the heads of revellers dripping with perfumes,[a]
          overcome with wine!

2   See, the Lord has one at his bidding, mighty and strong,
          whom he sets to work with violence against the land,
    like a sweeping storm of hail, like a destroying tempest,
    like a torrent of water in overwhelming flood.

3   The proud garlands of Ephraim's drunkards
         shall be trampled underfoot,

[a] revellers...perfumes: *prob. rdg., cp. Scroll; Heb.* a valley of fat things.

and the flowering sprays, so lovely in their beauty   4
    on the heads dripping with perfumes,[a]
shall be like early figs ripe before summer;
he who sees them plucks them,
and their bloom is gone while they lie in his hand.
On that day the LORD of Hosts shall be a lovely garland,   5
    a beautiful diadem for the remnant of his people,
a spirit of justice for one who presides in a court of   6
    justice,
and of valour for[b] those who repel the enemy at the gate.

These too are addicted to wine,   7
    clamouring in their cups:
priest and prophet are addicted to strong drink
    and bemused with wine;
clamouring in their cups, confirmed topers,[c]
    hiccuping in drunken stupor;
every table is covered with vomit,   8
    filth that leaves no clean spot.
Who is it that the prophet hopes to teach,   9
to whom will what they hear make sense?
Are they babes newly weaned, just taken from the
    breast?
It is all harsh cries and raucous shouts,   10
'A little more here, a little there!'
So it will be with barbarous speech and strange tongue   11
    that this people will hear God speaking,

[a] dripping with perfumes: *prob. rdg.*, *Scroll; Heb.* valley of fat
things.   [b] for: *prob. rdg.; Heb. om.*   [c] These too...topers: *or*
These too lose their way through wine and are set wandering by
strong drink: priest and prophet lose their way through strong drink
and are fuddled with wine; are set wandering by strong drink, lose
their way through tippling.

12   this people to whom he once said,
    'This is true rest; let the exhausted have rest.
    This is repose', and they refused to listen.
13   Now to them the word of the LORD will be
    harsh cries and raucous shouts,
    'A little more here, a little there!' –
    and so, as they walk, they will stumble backwards,
    they will be injured, trapped and caught.

✶ The first four verses contain an oracle against the northern kingdom anticipating the collapse of that kingdom at the hands of the invader, Assyria. Clearly it comes from the time when the northern kingdom was still in being, but disaster is imminent. Its leaders are like drunkards, utterly incapable of recognizing the national peril. The probability is that the oracle was first uttered during the reign of Hoshea (2 Kings 17: 1–6). Verse 2 refers to Assyria.

1. *the garlands* may be part of a spring festival, a celebration of a nature deity identified by the worshippers with Yahweh. This corruption of Yahweh-worship prevents their understanding of the work of the sovereign lord of history. So the oracle begins with a cry of distress (*Oh*), and continues with the threat (2–4).

4. The earlier *figs* came in May and were much prized for their delicacy, but they quickly withered.

5–6. These verses contain words of promise probably by a later disciple of Isaiah who looks to the day of the Lord as a restoration of a true order of society at the end of history.

7–13. Application of the earlier oracle to Judah, whose priests and prophets have also failed to recognize their danger. The specific mention of *priest and prophet* may indicate some kind of celebration in the temple in which it was believed that gratitude for God's gift of wine was best demonstrated by a *drunken* orgy. Isaiah would see this as a degradation of

Yahweh-worship and a basic cause of inability to form a right judgement in political affairs. Thus (9–10) they are unable to pay heed to Isaiah's word of the Lord. Verse 10 is difficult to reproduce in English. The first clause appears to be a double repetition of two Hebrew consonants as though they were mimicking a teacher teaching the abc. Then verse 11 suggests that the prophet's word of the Lord is like senseless babble; alternatively the word of the Lord can only now be recognized when the invader, speaking an unintelligible language, marches into the land. Having refused God's direction which assured them of security, they will be overcome by a foreign invader. ✻

THE VERDICT

Listen then to the word of the LORD, you arrogant men 14
who rule this people in Jerusalem.
You say, 'We have made a treaty with Death 15
  and signed a pact with Sheol:
so that, when the raging flood sweeps by, it shall not
    touch us;
  for we have taken refuge in lies
    and sheltered behind falsehood.'
These then are the words of the Lord GOD: 16
Look, I am laying a stone in Zion, a block of granite,
  a precious corner-stone for a firm foundation;
    he who has faith shall not waver.
I will use justice as a plumb-line 17
  and righteousness as a plummet;
hail shall sweep away your refuge of lies,
and flood-waters carry away your shelter.
Then your treaty with Death shall be annulled 18
and your pact with Sheol shall not stand;
the raging waters will sweep by,

and you will be like land swept by the flood.

19   As often as it sweeps by, it will take you;
morning after morning it will sweep by,
    day and night.
The very thought of such tidings
will bring nothing but dismay;

20   for 'The bed is too short for a man to stretch,
and the blanket too narrow to cover him.'

21   But the LORD shall arise as he rose on Mount Perazim
and storm with rage as he did in the Vale of Gibeon
to do what he must do – how strange a deed!
to perform his work – how outlandish a work!

22   But now have done with your arrogance,
lest your bonds grow tighter;
for I have heard destruction decreed
by the Lord GOD of Hosts for the whole land.

✳ This section begins with the charge against the rulers (verses 14–15), continues (verses 18–21) with the sentence passed on the guilty and ends with a solemn warning (verse 22) suggesting that even at this late hour there is time for repentance. Verses 16–17 appear to be a parenthetic reminder of what God has done.

15. *Death:* there is a word-play here, for the Hebrew word suggests both death and the Canaanite deity Môt. We might paraphrase: You have allied yourself with a dead god, instead of the living God; inevitably therefore he will bring you to the place of the dead (*Sheol*).

lies and *falsehood* signify in the prophetic speech, false gods who therefore deceive their worshippers.

16. Yet God is laying a firm foundation stone capable of supporting a great building and carved on it are the words, *he who has faith shall not waver* (cp. 7: 9).

17. The walls constructed of *righteousness* and *justice* will house a people securely when the storm beats upon that house. Disaster is the inevitable fate for those who rely on gods other than Yahweh.

20. This quotes a popular proverb: they have made their bed and must lie on it; but it is a poor bed with inadequate covering. *

LEARN FROM THE FARMER

Listen and hear what I say,	23
attend and hear my words.	
Will the ploughman continually plough for the sowing,	24
breaking his ground and harrowing it?	
Does he not, once he has levelled it,	25
broadcast the dill and scatter the cummin?	
Does he not plant the wheat in rows	
with barley*a* and spelt along the edge?	
Does not his God instruct him and train him aright?	26
Dill is not threshed with a sledge,	27
and the cartwheel is not rolled over cummin;	
dill is beaten with a rod,	
and cummin with a flail.	
Corn is crushed, but not to the uttermost,	28
not with a final crushing;	
his cartwheels rumble over it and break it up,	
but they do not grind it fine.	
This message, too, comes from the LORD of Hosts,	29
whose purposes are wonderful	
and his power great.	

[a] *Prob. rdg.; Heb. adds an unintelligible word.*

* There are two parables here, 23–6, ploughing and sowing; and 27–9, modes of threshing. No interpretation is given, and to an agricultural community none would be needed. Just as the farmer with ingrained wisdom and skill sows his seed and threshes the crops with careful discrimination, so God acts in history. There is nothing haphazard or indiscriminate about his acts. They are purposive and sensitive to people as they are. The parables had a particular application to the circumstances of Isaiah's day. The coming of the Assyrians spelt destruction, but within and beyond the suffering the divine work of redemption was being fulfilled. The wisdom of the farmer is from God; that divine wisdom is working in the larger field of Judah's history.

28. When the farmer threshes, the stalk and ear of the corn are *crushed* but the grain is shaken free. The divine purpose may seem to be defeated, but is in fact released.

It is evident that Isaiah was familiar with the characteristic modes of teaching as practised by the Wisdom teachers. The parable presents a familiar scene and encourages the hearers to think for themselves. *

BESIEGED BUT DELIVERED

29   Alas for Ariel! Ariel,
          the city where David encamped.
       Add year to year,
          let the pilgrim-feasts run their round,
2   and I will bring Ariel to sore straits,
       when there shall be moaning and lamentation.
       I will make her my Ariel indeed, my fiery altar.
3   I will throw my army round you like a wall;
       I will set a ring of outposts all round you
       and erect siege-works against you.
4   You shall be brought low, you will speak out of the
             ground

and your words will issue from the earth;
your voice will come like a ghost's from the ground,
and your words will squeak out of the earth.
Yet the horde of your enemies shall crumble into dust, 5
the horde of ruthless foes shall fly like chaff.
Then suddenly, all in an instant,
punishment shall come from the LORD of Hosts 6
with thunder and earthquake and a great noise,
with storm and tempest and a flame of devouring fire;
and the horde of all the nations warring against Ariel, 7
all their baggage-trains and siege-works,[a]
and all her oppressors themselves,
shall fade as a dream, a vision of the night.
Like a starving man who dreams 8
and thinks that he is eating,
but wakes up to find himself empty,
or a thirsty man who dreams
and thinks that he is drinking,
but wakes up to find himself thirsty and dry,
so shall the horde of all the nations be
that war against Mount Zion.

✻ This is a fine example of an earlier prophecy of doom being
modified by a later prophecy of salvation. It may be assumed
that the oracle of verses 1-4 was uttered at the beginning of
the Assyrian siege of Jerusalem (*Ariel*); then when everything
seemed hopeless, a further oracle was uttered (verses 5-8)
declaring God's purpose to destroy the enemy and deliver
Zion. The fulfilment of the earlier oracle by the siege of
Sennacherib will give confidence to the hearers that the second
oracle will be fulfilled. *Ariel* (verses 1, 2, 7) clearly means

[a] siege-works: *so Scroll; Heb.* strongholds.

Jerusalem. It is the same word as is used for *fiery altar*, a characteristic play on words by the prophet. The point then is that just as Jerusalem with its temple *altar* is the centre of the *pilgrim-feasts* with their great national sacrifices, so now the whole city will become like a burning altar as the invaders ravage and set it on fire. Suddenly the whole is reversed (5–8). The *fire* of the altar will break out against the invaders and they will flee in turn. The horrors of invasion will disappear, like a dream when the sleeper awakes. At the last moment, the hope expressed in the songs of Zion (cp. Ps. 48) will be realized.

If, as is possible, these oracles were uttered on the occasion of one of the great festivals, when such hymns were sung, the oracle would be doubly effective. *

BLIND LEADERS OF THE BLIND

9 Loiter and be dazed, enjoy yourselves and be blinded,
  be drunk but not with wine, reel but not with strong
      drink;

10 for the LORD has poured upon you a spirit of deep
      stupor;
    he has closed your eyes, the prophets,
    and muffled your heads, the seers.

11 All prophetic vision has become for you like a sealed
  book. Give such a book to one who can read and say,
  'Come, read this'; he will answer, 'I cannot', because it
12 is sealed. Give it to one who cannot read and say, 'Come,
  read this'; he will answer, 'I cannot read.'

* These verses, though reflecting the thoughts of 6: 9–10, are probably spoken to those who were planning rebellion in 705 B.C. The wilful disregard of the moral and spiritual claims of the sovereign Lord has made men incapable of under-

standing political reality. In such a people, the divine word of the prophet and the inspired wisdom of the wise man must be withheld. You do not cast pearls before swine. Verses 11–12 are in prose and may be the comment of a later disciple saddened by the failure of his generation to hear the words of the prophets. The educated who can read will not open the book; the uneducated who cannot are unable to receive the Word of the Lord. *

INSINCERE WORSHIP

Then the Lord said: 13

> Because this people approach me with their mouths
>> and honour me with their lips
> while their hearts are far from me,
> and their religion is but a precept of men, learnt by rote,
> therefore I will yet again shock this people, 14
>> adding shock to shock:
>> the wisdom of their wise men shall vanish
> and the discernment of the discerning shall be lost.

* It was the responsibility not only of prophets but of the 'wise' men to advise the king in matters of national policy. Human wisdom is not rejected merely because it is human, but because it is self-sufficient and failing in an awareness of the only ruler of history. The words for *shock* are used for divine acts of an extraordinary nature which clearly point men's minds to him. The use in Exod. 3: 20 ('miracles') and Exod. 15: 11 ('wonders') associates them with his saving work in the release from Egypt. In this passage they work against those who have forsaken God in spite of their religious language. The oracle would be appropriate to the beginning of the revolt against Assyria in 705 B.C. *

DOOM FOLLOWED BY RESTORATION

15   Shame upon those who seek to hide their purpose
            too deep for the LORD to see,
        and who, when their deeds are done in the dark,
        say, 'Who sees us? Who knows of us?'
16   How you turn things upside down,
        as if the potter ranked no higher than the clay!
        Shall the thing made say of its maker, 'He did not
                make me'?
        Shall the pot say of the potter, 'He has no skill'?
17   The time is but short
        before Lebanon goes back to grassland
        and the grassland is no better than scrub.
18   On that day deaf men shall hear
            when a book is read,
            and the eyes of the blind shall see
            out of impenetrable darkness.
19   The lowly shall once again rejoice in the LORD,
        and the poorest of men exult in the Holy One of Israel.
20   The ruthless shall be no more, the arrogant shall cease
                to be;
        those who are quick to see mischief,
21   those who charge others with a sin
        or lay traps for him who brings the wrongdoer into court
            or by falsehood deny justice to the righteous –
            all these shall be exterminated.

22   Therefore these are the words of the LORD the God of
    the house of Jacob, the God who ransomed Abraham:

        This is no time for Jacob to be shamed,

no time for his face to grow pale;
for his descendants will hallow my name 23
when they see*ᵃ* what I have done in their nation.
They will hallow the Holy One of Jacob
and hold the God of Israel in awe;
those whose minds are confused will gain 24
    understanding,
and the obstinate will receive instruction.

✶ In spite of Isaiah's words, the politicians continue to seek an alliance with Egypt against Assyria and ignore the clear guidance of God given by the prophet. For Isaiah, with his profound conviction that the Lord was at all times ruling the movement of history, this was wanton stupidity.

17. This appears to be an extended metaphor. *Lebanon*, famous all over the world for its proud cedars, will be reduced to cattle-grazing land, while old grazing grounds will revert to jungle. So will the proud be humbled. An alternative interpretation is to take verse 17 as introducing the words of verses 18–21, a picture of a reversal in the natural world which will be followed by a restoration of a true society. Verses 18ff. describe that reversal in human society when the humble will be exalted and the arrogant put to rout.

19–21. The theme appears in the Magnificat, Luke 1: 51–3.

22. *the God who ransomed Abraham:* no incident occurs in Genesis with which this reference could reasonably be associated, but there may have been traditions circulating orally which have not been included in the Old Testament. A later Jewish legend in Jubilees (a non-biblical Jewish book) speaks of Abraham being delivered from death by fire. Probably the reference in Isaiah is a somewhat unusual way of saying 'the people of God' such as is found in Isa. 41: 8; 51: 2. Many would regard this whole section as post-exilic. ✶

[a] *So Sept.; Heb.* he sees.

A FUTILE ALLIANCE

30   Oh, rebel sons! says the LORD,
       you make plans, but not of my devising,
       you weave schemes, but not inspired by me,
       piling sin upon sin;
2   you hurry down to Egypt without consulting me,
       to seek protection under Pharaoh's shelter
         and take refuge under Egypt's wing.
3   Pharaoh's protection will bring you disappointment
       and refuge under Egypt's wing humiliation;
4   for, though his officers are at Zoan
       and his envoys reach as far as Hanes,
5   all are left in sorry plight by that unprofitable nation,
       no help they find, no profit, only disappointment and
         disgrace.

✻ The oracle clearly refers to the attempt to gain security from the threat of Assyrian invasion by seeking an alliance with Egypt. Together with the oracles in verses 6–7, 8–14, 15–17 it belongs to the early part of 705–701 B.C. when the Judaean politicians were planning to rebel against Assyria. As a group of oracles they might be given the title 'A Covenant with Death' (see 28: 15). The alliance could be condemned politically, since Egypt was unable to defeat Assyria. The prophet condemns it on the grounds that negotiations had taken place without consulting God. Apparently a Judaean embassy was already on the way to Egypt (verse 2). Plans that ignore the Lord, the one ruler of history, are sure to bring disaster. (Pharaoh is no substitute for God.)

4. *Zoan*, or Tanis, is on the border of Egypt and Judah; *Hanes* or Anusis is in Middle Egypt. ✻

THE BEASTS OF THE SOUTH

The Beasts of the South: an oracle.   6

Through a land of hardship and distress
the tribes of lioness and roaring lion,
sand-viper and venomous flying serpent,
carry their wealth on the backs of asses
and their treasures on camels' humps
    to an unprofitable people.
Vain and worthless is the help of Egypt;   7
therefore have I given her this name,
    Rahab Quelled.

✻ The significance of the title at the beginning of verse 6 is
not clear. It is possible that it represents an experience in a
vision which is further described in the rest of the verse.
Apparently the Judaean envoys avoided, in the interests of
secrecy, the normal route through Philistine territory and took
the perilous route through the Negeb. This southern area,
because of its parched character, was regarded as a place of
lions, serpents and demons. So the Judaean envoys expose
themselves to all this danger for an alliance that will be useless
(*carry their wealth...to an unprofitable people*). The oracle
closes with a scathing epithet for *Egypt*. *Rahab*, in the ancient
myth, was the powerful and savage chaos monster that was
destroyed to make way for the ordered creation (cp. Ps. 74:
12–17). Egypt for all its apparent might is powerless. ✻

THE WRITTEN WARNING

Now come and write it on a tablet,   8
engrave it as an inscription before their eyes,
    that it may be there in future days,

a testimony for all time.

9   For they are a race of rebels, disloyal sons,
     sons who will not listen to the LORD's instruction;

10   they say to the seers, 'You shall not see',
     and to the visionaries, 'You shall have no true visions;
     give us smooth words and seductive visions.

11   Turn aside, leave the straight path,
     and rid us for ever of the Holy One of Israel.'

✳ This is a private oracle to the prophet himself. Once again, as in 8: 16, the prophet must write down the message that his people will not hear. How much was written on the tablet cannot be determined.

8. If it was written on *a tablet* or engraved *as an inscription*, it was a brief oracle such as might be scratched on a stone in the city wall. Such a brief oracle might then be verse 15. On the other hand the word for *inscription* commonly means a scroll, and what was written might then have been the series of oracles relating to Egypt. But the word for *engrave* would be inappropriate for writing on a scroll. The rendering in the N.E.B. is probably correct. In any case what is written will be an abiding witness, the truth of which would be only too apparent when the bitter lesson of history had been learned.

9. *disloyal sons:* i.e. they claim to be sons of God, but their actions deny this; cp. 1: 2.

10. Describes the effect of what they are saying. They wanted *the seers* to give a divine blessing to plans they had already made; they did not want to hear the harsh realities of Isaiah. Since his was the 'word of the Lord', they were in effect rejecting God. ✳

THE UNWELCOME TRUTH

These are the words of the Holy One of Israel: 12

    Because you have rejected this warning
    and trust in devious and dishonest practices,
      resting on them for support,
therefore you shall find this iniquity will be   13
      like a crack running down
    a high wall, which bulges
and suddenly, all in an instant, comes crashing down,
as an earthen jar is broken with a crash,   14
      mercilessly shattered,
    so that not a shard is found among the fragments
    to take fire from the glowing embers,
    or to scoop up water from a pool.

* The judge's sentence is pronounced: 'Because...therefore
...' It is presented in a vivid simile characteristic of an oriental
court. The simile may be prompted by the word for 'iniquity'
which has the meaning of 'not straight' or 'crooked', for
that is the way in which the crack would develop in a wall.
Then follows the total disintegration of the wall. If a city wall
is in mind, then the city is left defenceless, and the rubble is
good for nothing.

12. *devious* supposes a slight emendation of the Hebrew
'oppression'. *

JUDAH'S SUICIDAL POLICY

These are the words of the Lord GOD the Holy One of   15
Israel:

    Come back, keep peace, and you will be safe;
    in stillness and in staying quiet, there lies your strength.

16   But you would have none of it; you said, No,
          we will take horse and flee;
              therefore you shall be put to flight:
          We will ride apace;
              therefore swift shall be the pace of your pursuers.
17   When a thousand flee at the challenge of one,
          you shall all flee at the challenge of five, until you are
              left
          like a pole on a mountain-top, a signal post on a hill.

✸ 15. The passage opens with an oracle which is one of the
great utterances of Isaiah; it might be described as the living
heart of the prophet's teaching. It could have been spoken at
any time during the prophet's ministry, but was especially
appropriate to the frantic seeking for Egyptian help against
the Assyrian empire. *Come back:* i.e. to God whom you have
deserted. *keep peace:* i.e. to rely on him and his covenant-
promises to the dynasty of David. *you will be safe:* or, you
will be delivered. *in stillness and in staying quiet:* i.e. free from
anxiety and in whole-hearted trust in the source of all power.
This is at the heart of the whole biblical faith. The utter folly
of rejecting this is shown in the following verses. ✸

THE COMPASSIONATE GOD

18   Yet the LORD is waiting to show you his favour,
          yet he yearns to have pity on you;
              for the LORD is a God of justice.
          Happy are all who wait for him!

19   O people of Zion who dwell in Jerusalem, you shall
     weep no more. The LORD[a] will show you favour and
20   answer you when he hears your cry for help. The Lord

[a] *So Scroll; Heb. om.*

may give you bread of adversity and water of affliction, but he who teaches you shall no longer be hidden out of sight, but with your own eyes you shall see him always. If you stray from the road to right or left you shall hear 21 with your own ears a voice behind you saying, This is the way; follow it. You will reject, as things unclean, your 22 silvered images and your idols sheathed in gold; you will loathe them like a foul discharge and call them ordure.*a* The Lord will give you rain for the seed you sow, and 23 as the produce of your soil he will give you heavy crops of corn in plenty. When that day comes the cattle shall graze in broad pastures; the oxen and asses that work your 24 land shall be fed with well-seasoned fodder, winnowed with shovel and fork. On each high mountain and each 25 lofty hill shall be streams of running water, on the day of massacre when the highest in the land fall. The moon shall 26 shine with a brightness like the sun's, and the sun with seven times his wonted brightness, seven days' light in one, on the day when the LORD binds up the broken limbs of his people and heals their wounds.

* The picture presented here of the inhabitants of Jerusalem is so different from what precedes that the passage as a whole must come from a quite different situation. While verse 18 is in poetry, the remaining verses are in prose. These verses describe a people afflicted and in great need; there is no suggestion of a rebellious people.

18. *Yet* suggests a closer relationship with the preceding oracle than the Hebrew 'Therefore' would indicate. It is possible that, if Isaiah continued to prophesy after 701 B.C., this may be an oracle uttered after the disaster. It is more likely

[*a*] call them ordure: *or* say to them, Be off.

that it is an oracle of a prophet of a later date e.g. during the exile. The prose verses could be regarded as a commentary by one of the wise men who has reflected on the teaching of Isaiah.

20. Some commentators take *he who teaches you* as referring to God (so the Revised Standard Version), but the closing phrase makes it more likely that a human teacher is intended.

23–6. What follows describes the conditions of the Golden Age to come.

25. *on the day of massacre* appears to refer to the judgement on the enemies of the Lord's people which ushers in the new age. ✳

THE DIVINE INTERVENTION
AGAINST ASSYRIA

27   See, the name of the LORD comes from afar,
    his anger blazing and his doom heavy.
    His lips are charged with wrath
    and his tongue is a devouring fire.

28   His breath is like a torrent in spate,
      rising neck-high,
  a yoke to force the nations to their ruin,
  a bit in the mouth to guide the peoples astray.

29   But for you there shall be songs,
      as on a night of sacred pilgrimage,
  your hearts glad, as the hearts of men who walk to the
      sound of the pipe
  on their way to the LORD's hill, to the rock of Israel.

30   Then the LORD shall make his voice heard in majesty
  and show his arm sweeping down in fierce anger
      with devouring flames of fire,
  with cloudburst and tempests of rain and hailstones;

31   for at the voice of the LORD Assyria's heart fails her,

as she feels the stroke of his rod.

Tambourines and harps and shaking sistrums   32
    shall keep time
    with every stroke of his rod,
of the chastisement[a] which the LORD inflicts on her.
    Long ago was Topheth made ready,[b]   33
      made deep and broad,
    its fire-pit a blazing mass of logs,
    and the breath of the LORD like a stream of brimstone
      blazing in it.

✳ This prophecy may relate to the disaster that came to the Assyrian army referred to in 37: 36. A similar oracle occurs in 31: 4–9. The imagery of verses 27–8 is in conventional terms drawn from the liturgy (cp. Hab. 3: 3ff.; Ps. 18: 8–12).

29, 32. These verses appear to refer to the Passover festival at which the deliverance from Egypt was celebrated; this is a new Passover which will celebrate the deliverance from Assyria, whose doom is inevitable.

33. *Topheth:* the burning place is made ready (cp. Zeph. 1: 7). The place where the condemned sacrifices to Molech took place will be the place where the Assyrian will meet his doom.

It should be noted that the text of this passage is difficult. Some would suggest reading 27–8, 30 and follow with 29, 31–3. ✳

THE FOLLY OF THE APPEAL TO EGYPT

Shame upon those who go down to Egypt for help **31**
    and rely on horses,
putting their trust in chariots many in number

[a] *So some MSS.; others* foundation.
[b] *Prob. rdg.; Heb. adds* is that prepared also for the king?

and in horsemen in their thousands,
but do not look to the Holy One of Israel
or seek guidance of the LORD!

2   Yet the LORD too in his wisdom can bring about trouble
and he does not take back his words;
he will rise up against the league of evildoers,
against all who help those who do wrong.

3   The Egyptians are men, not God,[a]
their horses are flesh, not spirit;
and, when the LORD stretches out his hand,
the helper will stumble and he who is helped will fall,
and they will all vanish together.

✶ The historical situation is that of 30: 1–5. The distinctively oracular utterance is to be found in verses 1 and 3, while verse 2 reads like the prophet's own comment.

2. This is specifically addressed to the 'wise' counsellors who advocated this disastrous policy. With irony Isaiah would remind them that God is not lacking in *wisdom*; what is more to the point is that he can carry into effect the wise counsel he has offered. Their so-called wisdom is therefore dangerous folly. Those who persist in this foolish alliance are inviting disaster.

3. This sums up the argument, by contrasting the weakness (*flesh*) of the Egyptian forces with the illimitable energy (*spirit*) of God. They would do well to recall the words of the coronation hymn, Ps. 89: 21–3. ✶

ZION'S DEFENDER

4   This is what the LORD has said to me:

As a lion or a young lion growls over its prey
when the muster of shepherds is called out against it,

[a] Or gods.

and is not scared at their noise
or cowed by their clamour,
so shall the LORD of Hosts come down to do battle
for Mount Zion and her high summit.
Thus the LORD of Hosts, like a bird hovering over its 5
young,
will be a shield over Jerusalem;
he will shield her and deliver her,
standing over her and delivering her.
O Israel, come back to him whom you have so deeply 6
offended,
for on that day when you spurn, one and all, 7
the idols of silver and the idols of gold
which your own sinful hands have made,
Assyria shall fall by the sword, but by no sword of man; 8
a sword that no man wields shall devour him.
He shall flee before the sword,
and his young warriors shall be put to forced labour,
his officers shall be helpless from terror 9
and his captains too dismayed to flee.
This is the very word of the LORD
whose fire blazes in Zion,
and whose furnace is set up in Jerusalem.

---

* In two similes, Isaiah describes the Mighty Warrior. He is
like 'a lion' who will attack those who attempt to take from
him what is his, and like 'a bird' defending her fledglings.

6–7. This is like an interjection, a desperate appeal to Israel
to repent. It may have been prompted by the Hebrew word
for 'standing over' (verse 5) which resembles the word for
Passover.

7. This could be read as a future 'you shall spurn' and end

with a full-stop. The oracle continues in verse 8; Jerusalem will be delivered, as Israel was from Egypt or from the armies of Sisera (Judg. 4–5) by the power of God.

9. In the original this is obscure (cp. the Revised Standard Version) but the meaning is well represented in the N.E.B. *his officers*, literally 'his rock', which may refer to his army or his god. ✲

A RIGHTLY ORDERED SOCIETY

32   Behold, a king shall reign in righteousness
      and his rulers rule with justice,
2   and a man shall be a refuge from the wind
      and a shelter from the tempest,
        or like runnels of water in dry ground,
    like the shadow of a great rock in a thirsty land.
3   The eyes that can see will not be clouded,
      and the ears that can hear will listen;
4   the anxious heart will understand and know,
    and the man who stammers will at once speak plain.
5   The scoundrel will no longer be thought noble,
      nor the villain called a prince;
6   for the scoundrel will speak like a scoundrel
      and will hatch[a] evil in his heart;
        he is an impostor in all his actions,
    and in his words a liar even to the LORD;
        he starves the hungry of their food
        and refuses drink to the thirsty
7   The villain's ways are villainous
      and he devises infamous plans
      to ruin the poor with his lies

[a] *So Scroll; Heb.* do *or* conceal.

    and deny justice to the needy.

    But the man of noble mind forms noble designs   8

    and stands firm in his nobility.

✻ This passage is an adaptation and expansion of Wisdom teaching; cp. Prov. 20: 8, 26, 28. Although it is commonly read as future, it could be hypothetical 'When a king...then each shall be a refuge...' The former would make the passage similar to the Messianic passages of 9: 6–7; 11: 1–9. The latter would be teaching in the Wisdom mode but with an allusion to the coronation psalm 72. Since Isaiah has shown himself familiar with the Wisdom teaching of his day, there is no good reason for regarding this as a later addition. It may express his hopes for Hezekiah at the beginning of the reign, or his hopes for the future when the disasters had so fully justified his prophetic word.

    3. This verse picks up the thought of 6: 10; 29: 9 and reverses it.

    5–6. The *scoundrel* is the man who is morally insensitive and therefore depraved; the *villain*, a word only used here in the Old Testament, means a rascal or a knave; *impostor:* the noun occurs only here, but the corresponding verb means to be polluted and so alienated from God; a *liar* is one who brings confusion into society by his insincere speech. The whole passage describes a rightly ordered society in which evil conduct is seen for what it is and open-hearted generosity is recognized. ✻

COMPLACENT WOMEN

    You women that live at ease, stand up   9

        and hear what I have to say.

    You young women without a care, mark my words.

    You have no cares now, but when the year is out, you   10

        will tremble,

for the vintage will be over and no produce gathered in.

11   You who are now at ease, be anxious;
    tremble, you who have no cares.
    Strip yourselves bare;
    put a cloth round your waists
12   and beat your breasts[a]
    for the pleasant fields and fruitful vines.
13   On the soil of my people shall spring up thorns and
        briars,
    in[b] every happy home and in the busy town,
14   for the palace is forsaken and the crowded streets
        deserted;
    citadel[c] and watch-tower are turned into open heath,
    the joy of wild asses ever after and pasture for the flocks,

✶ This passage resembles that in 3: 16 – 4: 1, but is here directed not so much to the fashionable ladies of Jerusalem as to the *women* of the countryside. The living situation is that of the vintage harvest at the end of the year, an occasion of great merry-making at which also prayers were offered for a good and prosperous year to come. It was customary for the women to dance and sing at the harvest festival. But, like their menfolk, they were heedless of the threat of invasion in which their harvest will be pillaged or destroyed, and no men will be left to cultivate the ground. The once cultivated fields will be overrun with weeds, and the towns deserted. The women are summoned to ritual mourning. The oracle may have come from Isaiah's early ministry as in 3: 16ff., or the time of the Assyrian invasion in 701 when so much of the countryside was devastated. ✶

[a] and beat your breasts: *prob. rdg., cp. Scroll; Heb.* men beating the breast.
[b] *So Sept.; Heb.* because on.   [c] *Or* hill; *Heb.* Ophel.

RESTORATION

until a spirit from on high is lavished upon us.   15
   Then the wilderness will become grassland
   and grassland will be cheap as scrub;
   then justice shall make its home in the wilderness,   16
   and righteousness dwell in the grassland;
   when righteousness shall yield peace   17
and its fruit be quietness and confidence for ever.
   Then my people shall live in a tranquil country,   18
dwelling in peace, in houses full of ease;
   it will be cool on the slopes of the forest then,   19
   and cities shall lie peaceful in the plain.
   Happy shall you be, sowing every man by the   20
      water-side,
    and letting ox and ass run free.

* These verses appear to be an addition to the preceding. They present a picture of the age to come in which nature itself will respond to the establishment of righteousness and justice in society. Peace and security will reign; the pasturage will be so abundant that domestic animals will be able to graze freely.

15. *a spirit* may be misleading. What is meant is that divine power that is able to transform, recreate and bring new life.

19. This differs in the N.E.B. from earlier English Versions, but is possible and certainly suits the context. Earlier commentators had either to emend or treat the verse as misplaced. The passage as a whole resembles passages in the later chapters of the book.

The rest of this section (33: 1 – 35: 10) differs in both content and style from the oracles of Isaiah. Much of ch. 33 resembles the contents of the Psalter, while the contents of chs. 34 and 35 recall the conditions and hopes of the exile period. It is possible that earlier oracles of Isaiah have been used in a new historical situation and developed to meet the needs of that situation. If this is a right understanding of these chapters, we have a clear example of the way in which the prophet's words lived on to meet new needs. ✲

A PRAYER AND A PROMISE

33   Ah! you destroyer, yourself undestroyed,
        betrayer still unbetrayed,
        when you cease to destroy you will be destroyed,
        after all your[a] betrayals, you will be betrayed yourself.

2   O Lord, show us thy favour; we hope in thee.
        Uphold us[b] every morning,
        save us when troubles come.

3   At the roar of the thunder the peoples flee,
        at thy rumbling[c] nations are scattered;

4   their[d] spoil is swept up as if young locusts had swept it,
        like a swarm of locusts men swarm upon it.

5   The Lord is supreme, for he dwells on high;
        if you fill Zion with justice and with righteousness,

6   then he will be the mainstay of the age:[e]
        wisdom and knowledge are the assurance of salvation;
        the fear of the Lord is her[f] treasure.

✲ The passage falls into three parts: verse 1, an oracle of threat; 2–4, a prayer; 5–6, a word of assurance. It is in liturgical style. We may imagine a company of loyal Jews in the exilic or post-exilic age, led in their prayers by a prophet or priest.

[a] after all your; *so Scroll; Heb. unintelligible.* [b] *So some MSS.; others them.* [c] *So Scroll; Heb.* uplifting. [d] *Prob. rdg., cp. Targ.; Heb.* your. [e] the age: *prob. rdg.; Heb.* your times. [f] *Prob. rdg.; Heb.* his.

1. The *destroyer* is not named. There are points of resemblance to the words of Nahum's prophecy against Nineveh in 612, but he could be one of the later Persian kings during the time of the exile, after 587. A date as late as the Maccabean era is unlikely. The treacherous *destroyer* will suffer the fate he has inflicted on others (cp. 21: 2).

2–4. The prayer of the congregation, probably uttered by the leader. *Uphold us:* literally, be our arm. As so often in the prayers in the Psalter, prayer is offered in confidence that God will answer.

5–6. The leader speaks; the people are addressed. *if you fill:* the Hebrew has 'he has filled', the perfect tense suggesting the certainty of God's action. *the age:* the Hebrew has 'your times' and would suggest that the exalted Lord will give abiding stability to the great festivals where they would find him present. The closing phrase reflects the teaching of the wise. ✳

A LAMENT AND GOD'S ANSWER

Hark, how the valiant cry aloud for help,   7
    and those sent to sue for peace weep bitterly!
The highways are deserted, no travellers tread the roads. 8
Covenants are broken, treaties*a* are flouted;
        man is of no account.
    The land is parched and wilting,   9
    Lebanon is eaten away and crumbling;
    Sharon has become a desert,
    Bashan and Carmel are stripped bare.
Now, says the LORD, I will rise up.   10
Now I will exalt myself, now lift myself up.
What you conceive and bring to birth is chaff and   11
        stubble;

[a] *So Scroll; Heb.* cities.

187

a wind like fire shall devour you.

12   Whole nations shall be heaps of white ash,
or like thorns cut down and set on fire.

13   You who dwell far away, hear what I have done;
acknowledge my might, you who are near.

14   In Zion sinners quake with terror,
the godless are seized with trembling and ask,
Can any of us live with a devouring fire?
Can any live in endless burning?

15   The man who lives an upright life and speaks the truth,
who scorns to enrich himself by extortion,
who snaps his fingers at a bribe,
who stops his ears to hear nothing of bloodshed,
who closes his eyes to the sight of evil –

16   that is the man who shall dwell on the heights,
his refuge a fastness in the cliffs,
his bread secure and his water never failing.

✲ The lament is in 7–9; the Lord's answer in 10–13; the response of the congregation in 14–16.

The words of the lament suggest the same or a similar situation to that of verse 1. The opening words of verse 8 recall Judg. 5: 6. Verse 9, by referring to the most fertile districts, vividly describes the devastation. Verse 10 recalls the familiar words of the Psalms (Ps. 12: 5; 17: 13 etc.) where God arises to intervene on behalf of the needy. Verse 11 is apparently addressed to the enemy.

11. *a wind like fire:* The N.E.B. has divided a Hebrew word for 'your breath' following an ancient Jewish interpretation.

13. God's power will be universally acknowledged.

14–16. The congregational response recalls the familiar words of Ps. 15, a preparation for entering the holy temple. If verse 16 refers to Zion, it describes the guest of God receiving the food he provides. ✲

WORDS OF PROMISE

Your eyes shall see a king in his splendour   17
  and will look upon a land of far distances.
  You will call to mind what once you feared: 18
'Where then is he that counted, where is he that weighed,
  where is he that counted the treasures?'
  You will no longer see that barbarous people,   19
  that people whose speech was so hard to catch,
  whose stuttering speech you could not understand.

Look upon Zion, city of our solemn feasts,   20
  let your eyes rest on Jerusalem,
a land of comfort, a tent that shall never be shifted,
  whose pegs shall never be pulled up,
  not one of its ropes cast loose.
There we have the LORD's majesty;[a]   21
  it will be a place[b] of rivers and broad streams;
  but[c] no galleys shall be rowed there,
  no stately ship sail by.
For the LORD our judge, the LORD our law-giver,   22
the LORD our king – he himself will save us.
  [Men may say, Your rigging is slack;   23
  it will not hold the mast firm in its socket,
    nor can the sails be spread.]
Then the blind[d] man shall have a full share of the spoil
  and the lame shall take part in the pillage;
  no man who dwells there shall say, 'I am sick';   24
and the sins of the people who live there shall be
    pardoned.

[a] Or threshing-floor.   [b] it...place: or instead.   [c] Or and.
[d] Prob. rdg., cp. Targ.; Heb. obscure.

He has stretched across it a measuring-line of chaos,
　and its frontiers shall be a jumble of stones.

12　　No king shall be acclaimed there,
　and all its princes shall come to nought.

13　　Thorns shall sprout in its palaces;
　nettles and briars shall cover its walled towns.
It shall be rough land fit for wolves, a haunt of desert-
　　owls.

14　　Marmots shall consort with jackals,
　and he-goat shall encounter he-goat.
There too the nightjar shall rest
　and find herself a place for repose.

15　　There the sand-partridge shall make her nest,
　lay her eggs and hatch them
and gather her brood under her wings;
　there shall the kites gather,
　　one after another.

16　Consult the book of the LORD and read it:
　not one of these shall be lacking,
　　not one miss its fellow,
　for with his own mouth he has ordered it
　and with his own breath he has brought them together.

17　He it is who has allotted each its place,
　and his hand has measured out their portions;
　　they shall occupy it for ever
　　and dwell there from generation to generation.

* Although it is not likely that this chapter and the following came from the same prophet, each should be read in the light of the other. The final judgement of God must include the final defeat of all the forces of evil and the triumph of good. The language of this chapter is violent and terrifying, spoken

the heavens shall be rolled up like a scroll,
　and the starry host fade away,
as the leaf withers from the vine
　and the ripening fruit from the fig-tree;
for the sword of the LORD*ᵃ* appears*ᵇ* in heaven.　5
See how it descends in judgement on Edom,
on the people whom he dooms*ᶜ* to destruction.
The LORD has a sword steeped in blood,　6
　it is gorged with fat,
the fat of rams' kidneys, and the blood of lambs and
　　goats;
for he has a sacrifice in Bozrah,
a great slaughter in Edom.
Wild oxen shall come down and buffaloes*ᵈ* with them,　7
　bull and bison together,
and the land shall drink deep of blood
and the soil be sated with fat.
For the LORD has a day of vengeance,　8
the champion of Zion has a year when he will requite.
Edom's torrents shall be turned into pitch　9
　and its soil into brimstone,
and the land shall become blazing pitch,
　which night and day shall never be quenched,　10
　and its smoke shall go up for ever.
From generation to generation it shall lie waste,
and no man shall pass through it ever again.
Horned owl and bustard shall make their home in it,　11
screech-owl and raven shall haunt it.

[a] the sword of the LORD: *prob. rdg.; Heb.* my sword.　[b] *So Scroll; Heb.* drinks.　[c] *Prob. rdg.; Heb.* I doom.　[d] and buffaloes: *prob. rdg.; Heb. om.*

He has stretched across it a measuring-line of chaos,
and its frontiers shall be a jumble of stones.

12 No king shall be acclaimed there,
and all its princes shall come to nought.

13 Thorns shall sprout in its palaces;
nettles and briars shall cover its walled towns.
It shall be rough land fit for wolves, a haunt of desert-
owls.

14 Marmots shall consort with jackals,
and he-goat shall encounter he-goat.
There too the nightjar shall rest
and find herself a place for repose.

15 There the sand-partridge shall make her nest,
lay her eggs and hatch them
and gather her brood under her wings;
there shall the kites gather,
one after another.

16 Consult the book of the LORD and read it:
not one of these shall be lacking,
not one miss its fellow,
for with his own mouth he has ordered it
and with his own breath he has brought them together.

17 He it is who has allotted each its place,
and his hand has measured out their portions;
they shall occupy it for ever
and dwell there from generation to generation.

* Although it is not likely that this chapter and the following came from the same prophet, each should be read in the light of the other. The final judgement of God must include the final defeat of all the forces of evil and the triumph of good. The language of this chapter is violent and terrifying, spoken

WORDS OF PROMISE

Your eyes shall see a king in his splendour   17
    and will look upon a land of far distances.
    You will call to mind what once you feared: 18
'Where then is he that counted, where is he that weighed,
    where is he that counted the treasures?'
    You will no longer see that barbarous people,   19
    that people whose speech was so hard to catch,
    whose stuttering speech you could not understand.

Look upon Zion, city of our solemn feasts,   20
    let your eyes rest on Jerusalem,
a land of comfort, a tent that shall never be shifted,
    whose pegs shall never be pulled up,
    not one of its ropes cast loose.
There we have the LORD's majesty;*a*   21
    it will be a place*b* of rivers and broad streams;
    but*c* no galleys shall be rowed there,
    no stately ship sail by.
For the LORD our judge, the LORD our law-giver,   22
the LORD our king – he himself will save us.
    [Men may say, Your rigging is slack;   23
    it will not hold the mast firm in its socket,
    nor can the sails be spread.]
Then the blind*d* man shall have a full share of the spoil
    and the lame shall take part in the pillage;
    no man who dwells there shall say, 'I am sick';   24
and the sins of the people who live there shall be
    pardoned.

[a] *Or* threshing-floor.   [b] it...place: *or* instead.   [c] *Or* and.
[d] *Prob. rdg., cp. Targ.; Heb. obscure.*

* 17–19. Describes the restoration of the Davidic *king* in place of the foreign (? Persian) ruler. No longer will taxes be collected for the colonial power. Instead the true king will reign over the whole extent of the land (*far distances*) which David ruled.

20–2. Describes the restoration of *Jerusalem* and its temple. The restored city will have a perennial water-supply, apparently recalling Ezek. 47 and Ps. 46: 4. Unlike the waters of the Nile, the rivers are not for navigation, but for drinking and irrigation. The words of verse 22 recall the solemn shout in Ps. 46: 7, 11.

23*a*. This is quite obscure, and is only included here through its verbal association with verse 21. It is apparently an isolated fragment; even the translation is doubtful.

23*b*–4. The concluding sentences describe the enjoyment of God's victory so that even the disabled will have plenty. Sickness and sin will be done away. *

Edom and Israel

THE DAY OF JUDGEMENT

34   Approach, you nations, to listen,
             and attend, you peoples;
             let the earth listen and everything in it,
         the world and all that it yields;

2   for the LORD's anger is turned against all the nations
             and his wrath against all the host of them:
         he gives them over to slaughter and destruction.

3   Their slain shall be flung out,
         the stench shall rise from their corpses,
         and the mountains shall stream with their blood.

4   All the host of heaven shall crumble into nothing,

with the vigour and power of great poetry, and should be read as poetry. This is not to minimize the truth that it proclaims, but rather to emphasize that this is a theme that was taken with all seriousness by Israel's prophets as it was by Paul in Rom. 1: 18–32; cp. Matt. 25: 46. The poem in this chapter probably comes from the closing years of the exile and may be compared with Isa. 63: 1–6. It opens with a call to the whole world to see the divine wrath against all the peoples of the world. It is the final intervention of God against all that opposes his righteous purpose. The specific mention of *Edom* (verse 6) must be understood in relation to the cruel advantage taken by the Edomites of the Babylonian invasion of Judah in 598–587 B.C. referred to in Lam. 4: 21–2; Ps. 137: 7. But in this chapter *Edom* has become a symbolic name for all the enemies of the people of God, as it does in Obadiah. The prophet sees the whole universe as involved in the divine judgement; it is a return to primeval chaos. The poem may be divided into two movements; verses 2–8, the wrath of God is poured out; 9–17, the ruined earth.

8. *a day of vengeance:* the word in modern English distorts the meaning. The same language is used by Jesus in Luke 18: 5–8, where 'avenge' is translated 'vindicate' in the N.E.B. It has a positive as well as a negative meaning, putting right what is wrong and restoring the rights of one who is oppressed. Negatively it means the punishment of the evil-doer; positively it means the restoration of those who have suffered at his hands (cp. Isa. 35: 4). Since God is the only one who can justly and effectively do this, 'Vengeance is mine saith the Lord'. (The N.E.B. at Rom. 12: 19 has replaced 'vengeance' of earlier versions with 'justice'.)

9f. These verses pick up and magnify the picture of the destroyed cities of the plain in Gen. 19: 24f.

11. The land is abandoned to unclean creatures. *chaos... jumble* render the Hebrew words which in Gen. 1: 2 are rendered 'without form and void', i.e. a return to primeval chaos.

12. *No king shall be acclaimed there* could also be rendered mockingly 'They shall name it: No Kingdom There'.

13–15. These verses describe the once cultivated land reduced to desert, but it is possible that the wild creatures referred to may be names of demons e.g. satyr (*he-goat*) and Lilith (*nightjar*).

16–17. The meaning of these closing verses is not certain. *the book of the LORD* refers to that book in which are recorded the names of all his creatures (Ps. 139: 16; Dan. 12: 1; Mal. 3: 16). If these verses bring the preceding to a climax, they mean that the dreadful fate described is inescapable; it is eternally decreed. Alternatively they may, in contrast, indicate that when Edom's fate is accomplished the land shall once more be occupied by the Lord's people whose names are recorded in *the book* of life. The verses would then serve as a preparation for ch. 35. ✻

A GLAD RESTORATION

35 Let the wilderness and the thirsty land be glad,
    let the desert rejoice and burst into flower.

2 Let it flower with fields of asphodel,
    let it rejoice and shout for joy.
    The glory of Lebanon is given to it,
      the splendour too of Carmel and Sharon;
  these shall see the glory of the LORD, the splendour of
    our God.

3 Strengthen the feeble arms,
    steady the tottering knees;

4 say to the anxious, Be strong and fear not.
    See, your God comes with vengeance,
  with dread retribution he comes to save you.

5 Then shall blind men's eyes be opened,
    and the ears of the deaf unstopped.

Then shall the lame man leap like a deer,   6
  and the tongue of the dumb shout aloud;
for water springs up in the wilderness,
and torrents flow[a] in dry land.
The mirage becomes a pool,   7
  the thirsty land bubbling springs;
  instead of reeds and rushes, grass shall grow
  in the rough land where wolves now lurk.
And there shall be a causeway[b] there   8
which shall be called the Way of Holiness,
  and the unclean shall not pass along it;
it shall become a pilgrim's way,[c]
  no fool shall trespass on it.
No lion shall come there,   9
no savage beast climb on to it;
  not one shall be found there.
By it those he has ransomed shall return
  and the LORD's redeemed come home;   10
they shall enter Zion with shouts of triumph,
crowned with everlasting gladness.
Gladness and joy shall be their escort,
and suffering and weariness shall flee away.

* This poem also speaks of a day of vengeance, but here it is
the positive aspect that is described, the restoring of those who
have suffered grievously at the hands of the oppressor. The
exiles will be led home, not by the long caravan route, but
directly across the intervening desert. But it is a desert transformed into a Garden of Eden at the coming of the LORD to
lead them. The language was particularly meaningful to those

[a] flow: *so Scroll; Heb. om.* [b] *So Scroll; Heb. adds* and a road.
[c] a pilgrim's way: *prob. rdg.; Heb. unintelligible.*

who lived in that part of the world. *the desert* was no mere figure of speech. It was the place of death, where the shifting sand would from time to time uncover the bones of animals and men. It was hostile to all that was meant by the phrase 'the living God'. That was why the sins of Israel were symbolically driven away to the desert on the Day of Atonement. Now in the presence of the living God, the *glory*, all this is triumphantly transformed. There is also a further significance. Israel had its beginning in the exodus from Egypt and its wandering in the desert where the great revelation was received of the saving work and abiding presence of God. This will be a new exodus and a reborn Israel. A road from which the strongest might shrink will become a way along which the weakest and most fearful will walk with joyous confidence. So the prophet confidently looks to a return from the Babylonian exile. In his own day this was humanly speaking impossible; but his confidence was in the God who saves. So he describes those who will return as the pilgrims going to Zion to celebrate the great Festival of Tabernacles, ransomed, healed, restored, forgiven and singing the triumph-song. ✻

Jerusalem delivered from Sennacherib

✻ Chapters 36–9 are paralleled by 2 Kings 18: 13 – 20: 19, and since in Kings the sequence of thought is continuous with what precedes and follows, since also the style is characteristic of Kings, it may be assumed that the account in Isaiah was taken into the book from the Kings' account i.e. not earlier than a century after the events described.

There are, however, some differences. (1) The verses in 2 Kings 18: 14–16 are omitted after 36: 1. This may have been accidental. The first word of 2 Kings 18: 14 ('and he sent') is the same as that of 2 Kings 18: 17. In copying a manuscript, the eye of the scribe may have passed from the one verse to the other because the first word was identical. This is technically known as haplography. It is also possible that it was omitted (a) because it contains no reference to the prophet, and (b) because it was assumed to be a brief but parallel version of the following account. It so happens that these omitted verses correspond closely with the account of the same event in the annals of Sennacherib. There are some differences but they are hardly significant. (2) There are some minor differences between Isa. 36-9 and 2 Kings 18: 13-20: 19, the most obvious being the displacement of 2 Kings 20: 7-8; these verses have been restored to their original position in the N.E.B. But included in Isaiah is the psalm, Isa. 38: 9-20.

In the material common to both books there are considerable difficulties, and no one solution is completely satisfying. Whatever solution is adopted will affect the interpretation of those oracles of Isaiah that relate to this period of invasion. The starting-point must be with the verses in 2 Kings omitted in Isaiah. These correspond so closely with Sennacherib's account of the invasion of 701 B.C. and the surrender of Hezekiah, that they must be the Judaean account of the same event. In the material contained in Isaiah, we can recognize two accounts (a) Isa. 36: 2 – 37: 9a (to 'make war on him') to which 37: 36-8 would form a conclusion; and (b) 37: 9b-35. These could be regarded as two parallel accounts of the event described in 2 Kings 18: 14-16 but considerably expanded and certainly from different sources. Since Isaiah appears in both accounts they may well have come from circles of Isaianic disciples. Thus they contain both historical material and reflection. This would account for the differences in presentation. This suggestion is not without difficulty, the most obvious being the reference to the Nubian king, Tirhakah (37: 9). The extra-biblical records make it clear that, in 701, he was only nine years old and did not become king until after 690. This may be regarded as an anachronism, quite possible when the account was written some time after the events of 701.

An alternative view is to argue for a second invasion in about 689 B.C. in which the Assyrian army met the Egyptians under Tirhakah who had incited Hezekiah to rebel. The campaign was a failure from the Assyrian point of view and Sennacherib returned to Nineveh, where he was murdered in 681 B.C. Such an interpretation is entirely possible, but so far there is no evidence in the Assyrian records for this second campaign. Whatever the difficulties, therefore, we propose to regard the Isaiah passages as related to the brief statement in 2 Kings 18: 14–16 and Sennacherib's annals. Whatever historical interpretation is adopted for these chapters, the essential facts are as follows. (1) Hezekiah's policy reversed that of Ahaz. His religious reforms also implied a political modification, if not rejection, of his subservience to Assyria, a revival of the national religion. (2) This encouraged the belief that he would receive God's help in open revolt against his overlord. He might well have interpreted Isaiah's own oracles in this way (cp. Isa. 10: 24–7), although he ignored the prophet's warnings against dependence on Egypt. (3) His revolt led to the loss of a great deal of Judaean territory, and the payment of a crippling indemnity. If Sennacherib's annals are to be believed, many of the population were taken into exile as slaves. ✳

THE SIEGE OF JERUSALEM

36 1[a] IN THE FOURTEENTH[b] YEAR of the reign of Hezekiah, Sennacherib king of Assyria attacked and took all the
2 fortified cities of Judah. From Lachish he sent the chief officer[c] with a strong force to King Hezekiah at Jerusalem; and he halted by the conduit of the Upper Pool on the

[a] *Verses 1–22: cp. 2 Kgs. 18: 13–37: 2 Chr. 32: 1–19.*
[b] *Possibly an error for* twenty-fourth.   [c] *Or* sent Rab-shakeh.

causeway which leads to the Fuller's Field. There Eliakim 3
son of Hilkiah, the comptroller of the household, came
out to him, with Shebna the adjutant-general and Joah
son of Asaph, the secretary of state. The chief officer said 4
to them, 'Tell Hezekiah that this is the message of the
Great King, the king of Assyria: "What ground have
you for this confidence of yours? Do you*a* think fine 5
words can take the place of skill and numbers? On whom
then do you rely for support in your rebellion against me?
On Egypt? Egypt is a splintered cane that will run into 6
a man's hand and pierce it if he leans on it. That is what
Pharaoh king of Egypt proves to all who rely on him.
And if you tell me that you are relying on the LORD your 7
God, is he not the god whose hill-shrines and altars
Hezekiah has suppressed, telling Judah and Jerusalem that
they must prostrate themselves before this altar alone?"

'Now, make a bargain with my master the king of 8
Assyria: I will give you two thousand horses if you can
find riders for them. Will you reject the authority of even 9
the least of my master's servants and rely on Egypt for
chariots and horsemen? Do you think that I have come 10
to attack this land and destroy it without the consent of
the LORD? No; the LORD himself said to me, "Attack this
land and destroy it."'

Eliakim, Shebna, and Joah said to the chief officer, 11
'Please speak to us in Aramaic, for we understand it; do
not speak Hebrew to us within earshot of the people on
the city wall.' The chief officer answered, 'Is it to your 12
master and to you that my master has sent me to say this?
Is it not to the people sitting on the wall who, like you,

[a] *So Scroll, cp. Kgs. 18: 20; Heb.* I.

will have to eat their own dung and drink their own
13 urine?' Then he stood and shouted in Hebrew, 'Hear the
14 message of the Great King, the king of Assyria. These are
the king's words: "Do not be taken in by Hezekiah.
15 He cannot save you. Do not let him persuade you to rely on
the LORD, and tell you that the LORD will save you and
that this city will never be surrendered to the king of
16 Assyria." Do not listen to Hezekiah; these are the words
of the king of Assyria: "Make peace with me. Come out
to me, and then you shall each eat the fruit of his own
vine and his own fig-tree, and drink the water of his own
17 cistern, until I come and take you to a land like your own,
a land of grain and new wine, of corn and vineyards.
18 Beware lest Hezekiah mislead you by telling you that the
LORD will save you. Did the god of any of these nations
19 save his land from the king of Assyria? Where are the
gods of Hamath and Arpad? Where are the gods of
Sepharvaim? Where are the gods of Samaria?*a* Did they
20 save Samaria from me? Among all the gods of these
nations is there one who saved his land from me? And
how is the LORD to save Jerusalem.

21   The people were silent and answered not a word, for
the king had given orders that no one was to answer him.
22 Eliakim son of Hilkiah, comptroller of the household,
Shebna the adjutant-general, and Joah son of Asaph,
secretary of state, came to Hezekiah with their clothes
rent and reported what the chief officer had said.
37 1*b*   When King Hezekiah heard their report, he rent his
clothes and wrapped himself in sackcloth, and went into

[*a*] Where are the gods of Samaria?: *prob. rdg., cp. Luc. Sept. at 2 Kgs.
18: 34; Heb. om.*   [*b*] *Verses 1–38: cp. 2 Kgs. 19: 1–37; 2 Chr. 32: 20–2.*

the house of the LORD. He sent Eliakim comptroller of 2
the household, Shebna the adjutant-general, and the
senior priests, all covered in sackcloth, to the prophet
Isaiah son of Amoz, to give him this message from the 3
king: 'This day is a day of trouble for us, a day of reproof
and contempt. We are like a woman who has no strength
to bear the child that is coming to the birth. It may be 4
that the LORD your God heard the words of the chief
officer whom his master the king of Assyria sent to taunt
the living God, and will confute what he, the LORD your
God, heard. Offer a prayer for those who still survive.'
King Hezekiah's servants came to Isaiah, and he told them 5, 6
to say this to their master: 'This is the word of the LORD:
"Do not be alarmed at what you heard when the lackeys
of the king of Assyria blasphemed me. I will put a spirit 7
in him, and he shall hear a rumour and withdraw to his
own country; and there I will make him fall by the
sword."'

So the chief officer withdrew. He heard that the king 8
of Assyria had left Lachish, and he found him attacking
Libnah. But when the king learnt that Tirhakah king of 9*a*
Cush was on the way to make war on him...

* This is a fine example of Hebrew historical writing, vivid
and circumstantial in its details. It tells of the threat to
Jerusalem from the forces of Sennacherib, the report of the
propaganda speech delivered by the chief of staff, a mixture
of threat and persuasion which shows that the Assyrians were
well informed about Judaean affairs, the fears of Hezekiah
and the encouraging oracle of Isaiah. There is no indication
here that Hezekiah did in fact capitulate and pay a heavy
indemnity (2 Kings 18: 14–16).

1. *fourteenth year:* since the Assyrian invasion took place in 701 B.C. this assumes that Hezekiah came to the throne in 715 B.C. (The confusing figures in 2 Kings create difficulties about this date, and some have supposed that we should read 'twenty-fourth year', on the assumption that Hezekiah's reign began in about 726, as required by 2 Kings 18: 10.)

2. *Lachish:* a city about 40 metres (25 miles) south-west of Jerusalem. It was an important fortified city from the days of Solomon. A century after Isaiah's time it was besieged and destroyed by the Babylonians and a series of documents known as the Lachish Letters have been discovered among its ruins.

chief officer or *Rab-shakeh* (footnote) was a civilian of high rank accompanying the general. He would act here as the official spokesman of the Great King.

the conduit of the Upper Pool: cp. 7: 3, and the note there.

3. *Eliakim...Shebna:* cp. 22: 15–25.

4–10. This propaganda speech is well calculated to weaken morale, all the more that it was spoken in the language of the people (verse 11). Reliance upon Egypt was politically disastrous as events had shown. Isaiah had said as much (30: 1–5); the Assyrian drives it home with a homely figure of speech. Reliance on divine help was useless, because God was deeply offended by the profanation of his sanctuaries. This would be the view held by the Assyrians and by many of the Judaeans.

10. Here the Assyrian claims that God has commissioned him. This is not a pious phrase; the envoy could point to his successful campaign which in Judaean eyes could only have taken place with God's consent and support.

11. *Aramaic* was the language of international diplomacy, and, though akin to Hebrew, would be unintelligible to the ordinary Judaean. After the fifth century, it became the usual language even in Judaea, so that it was the mother tongue of Jesus.

12. *to eat...:* the conventional phrase to describe the effects of a siege.

16. They need no longer live on meagre rations, but eat the food they have stored before being taken into exile, which even so will not be a hardship.

19–20. The reference to Samaria is particularly effective. This was part of God's territory – the land of promise – which had become an Assyrian province twenty years before.

37: 1–2. *Hezekiah*, mourning what appeared to be inevitable disaster, went to the temple to seek divine guidance, and sent his senior officials to the prophet whose words he had hitherto ignored.

4. *Offer a prayer:* note the function of the prophet as intercessor.

6. The reply of the prophet hardly indicates the capitulation of Hezekiah in 2 Kings 18: 14–16. It may be assumed that a century later the disaster was forgotten in the evident fact that Jerusalem was not actually captured and that Hezekiah continued to reign.

7. *I will put a spirit in him.* We should probably say that Sennacherib suddenly changed his mind. But in the ancient world this would be seen as divine action. The *rumour* would be news of rebellion in Mesopotamia, probably in Babylon. *fall by the sword:* this did not in fact happen until twenty years after the siege of Jerusalem, i.e. in 681 B.C.

8. *Libnah* is some 16 metres (10 miles) north of *Lachish*.

9a. If the sentence continues to the end of the verse, *when* is necessary in English, but is not expressed in Hebrew. The sentence could end at *on him*. *Tirhakah* became king of Ethiopia (*Cush*) and Egypt from 690 to 664 B.C. He was about nine years old at the time of the siege of Jerusalem. ✳

THE THREAT TO JERUSALEM AND
PROMISE OF DELIVERANCE

He sent messengers again[a] to Hezekiah king of Judah, 9*b*

[a] again: *prob. rdg., 2 Kgs. 19: 9; Heb.* and he heard.

10 to say to him, 'How can you be deluded by your god on whom you rely when he promises that Jerusalem shall not
11 fall into the hands of the king of Assyria? Surely you have heard what the kings of Assyria have done to all countries, exterminating their people; can you then hope to escape?
12 Did their gods save the nations which my forefathers destroyed, Gozan, Harran, Rezeph, and the people of Beth-
13 eden living in Telassar? Where are the kings of Hamath, of Arpad, and of Lahir, Sepharvaim, Hena, and Ivvah?'

14 Hezekiah took the letter from the messengers and read it; then he went up into the house of the LORD, spread it
15, 16 out before the LORD and offered this prayer: 'O LORD of Hosts, God of Israel, enthroned on the cherubim, thou alone art God of all the kingdoms of the earth; thou hast
17 made heaven and earth. Turn thy ear to me, O LORD, and listen; open thine eyes, O LORD, and see; hear the message
18 that Sennacherib has sent to taunt the living God. It is true, O LORD, that the kings of Assyria have laid waste
19 every country,*a* that they have consigned their gods to the fire and destroyed them; for they were no gods but
20 the work of men's hands, mere wood and stone. But now, O LORD our God, save us from his power, so that all the kingdoms of the earth may know that thou, O LORD, alone art God.'*b*

21 Isaiah son of Amoz sent to Hezekiah and said, 'This is the word of the LORD the God of Israel: I have heard*c* your prayer to me concerning Sennacherib king of
22 Assyria. This is the word which the LORD has spoken concerning him.'

[*a*] *So Scroll; Heb. adds* and their country.   [*b*] God: *so Scroll and 2 Kgs. 19: 19; Heb. om.*   [*c*] I have heard: *so Sept. and 2 Kgs. 19: 20; Heb. om.*

The virgin daughter of Zion disdains you,
> she laughs you to scorn;
the daughter of Jerusalem tosses her head
> as you retreat.

> Whom have you taunted and blasphemed?   23
> Against whom have you clamoured,
casting haughty glances at the Holy One of Israel?

> You have sent your servants to taunt the Lord,   24
> and said:

With my countless chariots I have gone up
high in the mountains, into the recesses of Lebanon.
I have cut down its tallest cedars,
> the best of its pines,
I have reached its highest limit of forest and meadow.*a*

> I have dug wells   25
and drunk the waters of a foreign land,*b*
and with the soles of my feet I have dried up
> all the streams of Egypt.

> Have you not heard long ago?   26
> I did it all.

In days gone by I planned it
and now I have brought it about,
making fortified cities tumble down
> into heaps of rubble.*c*

Their citizens, shorn of strength,   27
> disheartened and ashamed,
were but as plants in the field, as green herbs,
as grass on the roof-tops blasted before the east wind.*d*

[*a*] and meadow: *prob. rdg.; Heb.* its meadow.   [*b*] of a foreign land:
so Scroll and 2 Kgs. 19: 24; Heb. om.   [*c*] rubble: *so Scroll; Heb. obscure.*
[*d*] blasted...east wind: *so Scroll; Heb. obscure.*

28   I know your rising up[a] and your sitting down,
          your going out and your coming in.

29   The frenzy of your rage against me[b] and your arrogance
          have come to my ears.
          I will put a ring in your nose
          and a hook in your lips,
          and I will take you back by the road
          on which you have come.

30   This shall be the sign for you: this year you shall eat shed
      grain and in the second year what is self-sown; but in the
      third year sow and reap, plant vineyards and eat their

31   fruit. The survivors left in Judah shall strike fresh root

32   under ground and yield fruit above ground, for a remnant
      shall come out of Jerusalem and survivors from Mount
      Zion. The zeal of the LORD of Hosts will perform this.

33   'Therefore, this is the word of the LORD concerning the
      king of Assyria:

          He shall not enter this city
              nor shoot an arrow there,
          he shall not advance against it with shield
              nor cast up a siege-ramp against it.

34   By the way on which he came he shall go back;
          this city he shall not enter.
          This is the very word of the LORD.

35   I will shield this city to deliver it,
          for my own sake and for the sake of my servant David.'

36   The angel of the LORD went out and struck down a
      hundred and eighty-five thousand men in the Assyrian

37   camp; when morning dawned, they all lay dead. So

[a] your rising up: *so Scroll; Heb. om.*
[b] *So Scroll; Heb. repeats* the frenzy of your rage against me.

Sennacherib king of Assyria broke camp, went back to
Nineveh and stayed there. One day, while he was wor-   38
shipping in the temple of his god Nisroch, Adrammelech
and Sharezer his sons murdered him and escaped to the
land of Ararat. He was succeeded by his son Esarhaddon.

* This section is sufficiently parallel to the preceding to
justify the suggestion that it comes from another circle of
Isaiah's disciples. It is of importance in that it contains
Hezekiah's prayer, and two oracles of Isaiah. It may be noted
that certain obscurities in the text have been eased by the
discovery of the Dead Sea scrolls of Isaiah, cp. the N.E.B.
footnotes.

10–13. The tone of the Assyrian message is different here.
The God of *Hezekiah* is unable to help, and is no more
competent than the gods of the cities and states of Mesopotamia and Syria. Here we have a direct challenge to God
himself.

14. This is the first mention of a *letter*; it is assumed that it
contained the text of what the *messengers* said.

16–20. These verses use the conventional language of
temple prayers, insert the statement of the particular occasion,
and confidently expect an answer. *enthroned on the cherubim*
is a reference to the ark-throne and unseen powers which these
figures represent.

21–9. Contains the answer to Hezekiah's prayer through
the prophet. It is an oracle cast in the form of a funeral dirge
over *Sennacherib* and so corresponds to 37: 7; he is as good
as dead! It is thus a taunt-song like 10: 5–16. Although the
Great King has boasted of his conquests (22–5) his acts were
but the fulfilment of God's purpose. His arrogance has earned
the shame and ignominy that will come. He will be caught
like a wild animal and driven back to his homeland.

30–2. This is a prose oracle assuring Hezekiah that, though
his people will suffer hardship for two years, in the third year

their life will return to normal. *shed grain* is that which falls in the fields in the process of reaping; *self-sown* or wild grain.

33–5. An oracle foretelling the departure of Sennacherib. It might have originally followed verse 21, as the word *Therefore* would suggest. It must have been uttered before the siege began since it declares (verse 33) that Sennacherib will retreat without besieging the city.

36–8. This is probably the conclusion of the earlier account. It must be admitted that no such disaster is recorded in any known Assyrian records. There is a story recorded by Herodotus of a plague of mice which gnawed the bow-strings of Sennacherib's soldiers when they were attacking Egypt. But the resemblance to verse 36 is not close. The biblical account describes a plague, understood as a divine visitation, which caused *Sennacherib* to return to Nineveh. Verse 38 records the murder of Sennacherib in 681 B.C. by his sons, whose names do not appear in the Assyrian inscriptions. He was succeeded by *Esarhaddon*, who was not implicated in the murder. *Nisroch* is unknown; it may be a Hebrew misunderstanding for Nusku, the fire-god. *Ararat* is Armenia. ✷

HEZEKIAH'S ILLNESS AND RECOVERY

38 1[a] At this time Hezekiah fell dangerously ill and the prophet Isaiah son of Amoz came to him and said, 'This is the word of the LORD: Give your last instructions to your household, for you are a dying man and will not
2 recover.' Hezekiah turned his face to the wall and offered
3 this prayer to the LORD: 'O LORD, remember how I have lived before thee, faithful and loyal in thy service, always doing what was good in thine eyes.' And he wept
4, 5 bitterly. Then the word of the LORD came to Isaiah: 'Go and say to Hezekiah: "This is the word of the LORD the

[a] *Verses 1–8, 21, 22: cp. 2 Kgs. 20: 1–11.*

God of your father David: I have heard your prayer and
seen your tears; I will add fifteen years to your life. I will 6
deliver you and this city from the king of Assyria and will
protect this city."' Then Isaiah told them to apply a fig- 21^{*a*}
plaster; so they made one and applied it to the boil, and
he recovered. Then Hezekiah said, 'By what sign shall I 22
know that I shall go up into the house of the LORD?' And 7
Isaiah said,^{*b*} 'This shall be your sign from the LORD that
he will do what he has promised. Watch the shadow 8
cast by the sun on the stairway of Ahaz: I will bring back-
wards ten steps the shadow which has gone down on the
stairway.' And the sun went back ten steps on the stairway
down which it had gone.

A poem of Hezekiah king of Judah after his recovery 9
from his illness, as it was written down:

I thought: In the prime of life I must pass away;   10
    for the rest of my years I am consigned to the gates of
        Sheol.
  I said: I shall no longer see the LORD   11
    in the land of the living;
  never again, like those who live in the world,^{*c*}
    shall I look on a man.
  My dwelling is taken from me,   12
    pulled up like a shepherd's tent;
  thou hast cut short^{*d*} my life like a weaver
  who severs the web from the thrum.
  From morning to night thou tormentest me,
    then I am racked with pain^{*e*} till the morning.   13

[*a*] *Verses 21, 22 transposed.*   [*b*] And Isaiah said: *prob. rdg., cp.* 2 Kgs.
20: 9; Heb. om.   [*c*] world: *so some MSS.; others* cessation.   [*d*] *Prob.
rdg., cp. Scroll; Heb.* I have gathered.   [*e*] then...pain: *so Scroll; Heb.*
I wait.

All my bones are broken, as a lion would break them;
from morning to night thou tormentest me.

14   I twitter as if I were a swallow,[a]
    I moan like a dove.
My eyes falter as I look up to the heights;
O Lord, pay heed, stand surety for me.

15   How can I complain, what can I say to the LORD[b]
    when he himself has done this?
I wander to and fro all my life long
in the bitterness of my soul.

16   Yet, O Lord, my soul shall live with thee;
do thou give my spirit rest.[c]
Restore me and give me life.

17   Bitterness had indeed been my lot in place of
    prosperity;
but thou by thy love hast brought me back
from the pit of destruction;
for thou hast cast all my sins behind thee.

18   Sheol cannot confess thee,
Death cannot praise thee,
nor can they who go down to the abyss
hope for thy truth.

19   The living, the living alone can confess thee
as I do this day,
as a father makes thy truth known, O God, to his sons.

20   The LORD is at hand to save me;
so let us sound the music of our praises
all our life long in the house of the LORD.[d]

[a] *So Sept.; Heb. adds* a wryneck.   [b] *Prob. rdg., cp. Targ.; Heb.* what can he say to me.   [c] Yet...rest: *prob. rdg.; Heb. unintelligible.*
[d] *Verses 21, 22 transposed to follow verse 6.*

✷ The account is somewhat abbreviated from 2 Kings 20: 1–11, but includes the thanksgiving psalm of Hezekiah, not found in Kings. There is no obvious connection between the king's illness and the threat to Jerusalem except in verse 1 'At this time' and the promise of protection for the city in verse 6. The reference in 39: 1 to the embassy from Babylon would suggest that the visit took place before the rebellion had started, if not before the earlier unrest in 711 B.C.

1. *At this time* is a very general phrase and could be rendered 'in those days'. There is no attempt to connect Hezekiah's illness with any specific sin, and Hezekiah's prayer in verse 3 does not suggest penitence for such rebellious acts against God as Isaiah had described in 29: 13f. or 31: 1. It may, however, be said that the anxieties of the king during the earlier part of his reign might well have resulted in this physical affliction. We should think of an ulcer rather than a boil; his condition was so serious that he had no hope of recovery. Indeed Isaiah told him that death was imminent.

3. The prayer is not a penitential prayer, but a plea for help appropriate from one who had done 'what was right in the eyes of the LORD' and 'did not fail in his allegiance to him' (2 Kings 18: 3, 6).

5. *Isaiah* then returned to *Hezekiah* with an assurance that he would recover and live a further *fifteen years*.

21. Isaiah instructed that a fomenting *plaster* be applied to drain the ulcer.

7–8. Then followed a sign (verses 7–8 are a somewhat abbreviated form of 2 Kings 20: 9–11). The Hebrew text is not very clear but it would appear that there was a building which Ahaz had introduced, perhaps an altar with steps (2 Kings 16: 12). On these steps *the sun* cast a *shadow* from some part of another building (the royal palace?). It was not a sun-dial (as in earlier English Versions), but it could serve to mark the passage of time. The sign was that the shadow would recede *ten steps* to an earlier position. It is impossible to think of any natural phenomenon to account for this. Even refraction caused by unequally heated layers of air would hardly produce so great an effect. If a rationalistic explanation should be sought, it might be suggested that what was originally a much smaller effect has been magnified in the process of time. A further difficulty lies in the number *ten*. We should have expected a number to correspond to the addition of 'fifteen' years to Hezekiah's life.

9–20. The poem of Hezekiah is a liturgical psalm, an individual thanksgiving to be used, accompanied by a sacrifice, on recovery from an illness (cp. Pss. 6, 38). In verse 9 the N.E.B. seems to have rendered the same word twice, *poem* (by a small emendation) and *as it was written down*. Since this verse is a title, as in Pss. 56–60 (see the Authorized Version), the former should be retained. It is a title for psalms of expiation. The psalm may be divided into two main sections. Verses 10–14 record the condition from which the sufferer needs to be saved. Verses 15–20 contain the appeal to God for help. Death appears to be inevitable, and that meant, until a late period of Judaism, separation from God and from the covenant people. This is the sting of death. Sheol was the dark abode where all activity ceased (cp. 18–19). As the place of the dead, it was the negation of the living God.

14. *stand surety for me:* an appeal to God from the debtor to be his security lest he be condemned to prison; cp. Job 17: 3.

15. It was accepted that sickness was an act of God, presumably on account of some misdeed, but therefore God could heal. Forgiveness of sin and recovery from illness went together in God's saving purpose.

19. Recovery has already taken place and the psalm ends in a great burst of praise. ✶

THE BABYLONIAN ENVOYS

At this time Merodach-baladan son of Baladan king of **39** 1[a]
Babylon sent envoys with a gift to Hezekiah; for he had
heard that he had been ill and was well again. Hezekiah 2
welcomed them and showed them all his treasury, silver
and gold, spices and fragrant oil, his entire armoury and
everything to be found among his treasures; there was
nothing in his house and in all his realm that Hezekiah
did not show them. Then the prophet Isaiah came to 3
King Hezekiah and asked him, 'What did these men say
and where have they come from?' 'They have come
from a far-off country,' Hezekiah answered, 'from
Babylon.' Then Isaiah asked, 'What did they see in your 4
house?' 'They saw everything,' Hezekiah replied; 'there
was nothing among my treasures that I did not show
them.' Then Isaiah said to Hezekiah, 'Hear the word of 5
the LORD of Hosts: The time is coming, says the LORD, 6
when everything in your house, and all that your forefathers have amassed till the present day, will be carried
away to Babylon; not a thing shall be left. And some of 7
the sons who will be born to you, sons of your own
begetting, shall be taken and shall be made eunuchs in
the palace of the king of Babylon.' Hezekiah answered, 8
'The word of the LORD which you have spoken is good',
thinking to himself that peace and security would last
out his lifetime.

☆ It is evident that this visit was more than a courtesy visit. It could not have taken place during the siege of Jerusalem,

[a] *Verses 1–8: cp. 2 Kgs. 20: 12–19.*

nor, from the amount of treasure displayed, after the capitulation. Merodach-baladan is a Hebraised form of Marduk-apal-iddina, with the name of the god Marduk given the vowels of the Hebrew word 'accursed'. He ruled in Babylon from 720 to 709, was driven out by Sargon, but returned briefly in 704/3. The most probable date for the visit would be 711 when there were wide-spread revolts in the Assyrian empire. Clearly the aim was to incite Hezekiah to rebel so as to divide the Assyrian forces. The statement that Hezekiah *showed them all his treasury* would mean in modern English that he revealed his economic resources as well as his military might.

Isaiah was clearly aware that a military alliance was envisaged; already Hezekiah was recognized as a leading figure among the small nations of south-west Asia, and hoping for Egyptian support. Isaiah had always condemned such military adventures. These political alliances were an implied rejection of Yahweh, the sovereign Lord of history; such alliances were certain to fail. There is good reason to accept the substantial historicity of this event, though some of the details may need correction.

1. *son of Baladan*. The name of the father was Yakin. *Baladan* is an impossible name; presumably the writer misunderstood the form of the Babylonian king's name. *a gift:* visits from one king to another always included an exchange of gifts as a mark of fellowship.

2. *spices and fragrant oil* suggest that Hezekiah engaged in trade through the Gulf of Aqaba.

5-7. Doubtless based on an original oracle, perhaps Nineveh was referred to by the prophet instead of Babylon. This actually happened in 701. Probably Babylon was substituted here at a later date when, after the fall of Jerusalem in 586, the wealth of the city and the royal family were taken to Babylonia.

8. These words seem strange in English. But they well represent the acceptance by the king of a divine word, even if it be a word of doom. The final sentence, though hardly

adequate to a true worshipper of God, simply indicates that the future is unknown but that at present all is well.

This part of the book of Isaiah ends on a sombre note, as indeed the eighth century B.C. did. But these words were not written by a historian coolly recording past events. They were written by one who dared to believe that Israel had a future in spite of the apparently irretrievable disaster of the exile. So he wrote of what had happened and how men behaved in order that, in that future, men would learn from the past and begin life anew in loyal trust and obedience.

✳   ✳   ✳   ✳   ✳   ✳   ✳   ✳   ✳   ✳   ✳   ✳   ✳

A NOTE ON FURTHER READING

The commentaries by G. B. Gray, *Isaiah I–XXVII, International Critical Commentary* (T. & T. Clark, 1912) and E. J. Kissane, *The Book of Isaiah I* (Browne and Nolan, 1941) pre-suppose a knowledge of Hebrew for understanding the text. Other commentaries that will be found useful are G. W. Wade, *Isaiah, Westminster Commentaries* (2nd edition, 1929), J. Mauchline, *Isaiah 1–39, Torch Bible Commentaries* (S.C.M., 1962). Valuable background material will be found in G. W. Anderson, *The History and Religion of Israel, New Clarendon Bible* (O.U.P., 1966), B. W. Anderson, *The Living World of the Old Testament* (2nd edition, Longmans, 1967), E. W. Heaton, *The Hebrew Kingdoms, New Clarendon Bible* (O.U.P., 1968). A detailed analysis of these chapters may be found in O. Eissfeldt, *The Old Testament, an Introduction* (Blackwell, 1965). A discussion of the difficult problems relating to the Assyrian invasion of Judah may be found in B. S. Childs, *Isaiah and the Assyrian Crisis* (S.C.M., 1967). J. Pritchard, *Ancient Near Eastern Texts Relating to the Old Testament* (third edition, Princeton, 1969) and D. Winton Thomas (ed.), *Documents from Old Testament Times* (Oliver and Boyd, Harper, 1958) both contain the texts of contemporary documents.

Other books, mentioned in the commentary, are: G. von Rad, *Old Testament Theology* (2 vols., Harper, 1962–5), J. H. Eaton, *Psalms* (S.C.M., 1967) and A. R. Johnson, *Sacral Kingship in Ancient Israel* (revised edition, University of Wales, 1967).

INDEX